Building Brains

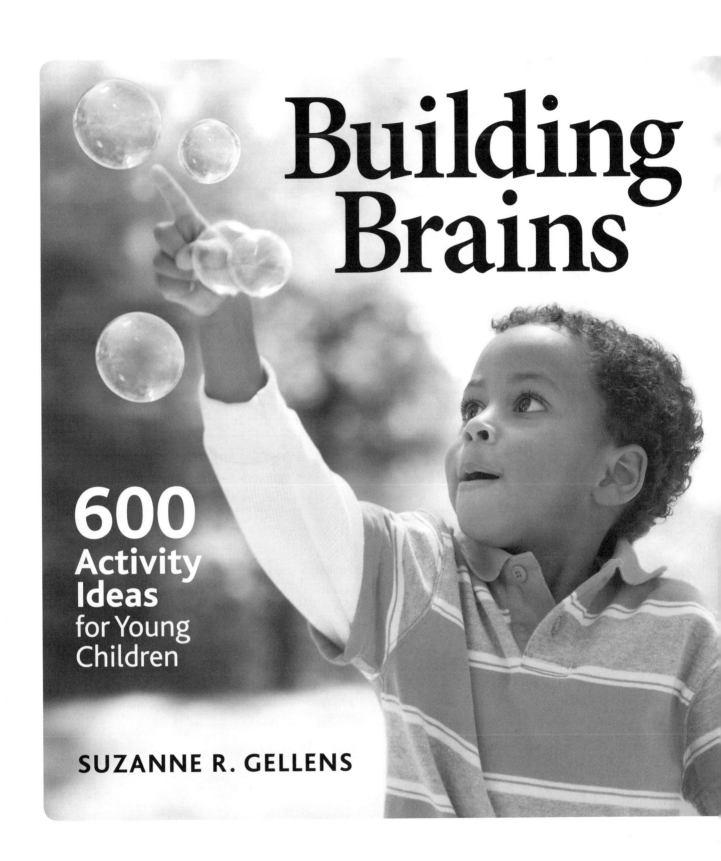

Building Brains

600
Activity
Ideas
for Young
Children

SUZANNE R. GELLENS

Redleaf Press®
www.redleafpress.org
800-423-8309

Published by Redleaf Press
10 Yorkton Court
St. Paul, MN 55117
www.redleafpress.org

First edition 2013
Cover design by Jim Handrigan
Cover photograph © Blend Images Photography/Veer
Interior design by Percolator
Typeset in FF Celeste and Bliss
Illustration on page 8 by Shawn Thomas
Printed in the United States of America
19 18 17 16 15 14 13 12   1 2 3 4 5 6 7 8

An earlier version of this book was published as *Activities That Build the Young Child's Brain,* © 2007 by Suzanne R. Gellens.

The tips for preventing sudden infant death syndrome (SIDS) on pages 55–56 were originally published in the online article "Reducing the Risk of SIDS" by the American SIDS Institute; www.sids.org/nprevent.htm. Reprinted with permission.

Library of Congress Cataloging-in-Publication Data
Gellens, Suzanne.
    Building brains : 600 activity ideas for young children / Suzanne R. Gellens.
       p. cm.
    Includes bibliographical references and index.
    Summary: "Building Brains expands young children's learning with six hundred brain-based, developmentally appropriate activity ideas. It combines the latest information on brain development with activities that support children's learning and enrich any early childhood curriculum."
    — Provided by publisher.
    ISBN 978-1-60554-117-4 (pbk.)
    1. Early childhood education—Activity programs. 2. Creative activities and seat work
    3. Child development. 4. Learning, Psychology of.   I. Title.
    LB1139.35.A37G46 2012
    372.21—dc23   621 2521
                    2012007940

This book is dedicated to the memory of my husband, Paul, who listened to me as I talked through the book, and to the memory of Beth Moore, my dear friend and administrative assistant, who typed and formatted multiple versions of the book and helped me translate my ideas into coherent sentences.

Contents

Acknowledgments

Over the years, I have read books and attended numerous conferences and workshops. Often I would go back to the classroom and try out the ideas and modify them to fit my teaching style. The activity became part of my repertoire, and I made it my own. I changed the focus to meet the needs of the children I was teaching at the time. I owe a debt of gratitude to the many people who originated the ideas and gave me the flexibility to adapt them to use with the children in my classes.

I have been fortunate to have many mentors. They are too many to list, but to each of you I say thank you for giving me the strength, knowledge, and courage to forge ahead and try new avenues. You helped me hone the attributes to be a leader, and for this I am extremely grateful. You encouraged me to succeed on every level I tried and let me know that I could expand my horizons even more.

Thank you to the many people who aided me in completing this book. I am indebted to many leaders in the Florida Association for the Education of Young Children who gave me content suggestions, proofread the document, and pointed out errors in organization and grammar. I am grateful to my children and three grandchildren for letting me watch them grow and develop. These observations renewed my interest in and wonder at this process called learning. Thank you also to the staff members at Temple Emanu-El Early Learning Center in Sarasota, Florida, for giving me a place to initiate my ideas and to Dr. Bernard Maria, whose friendship, knowledge of brain development, and guidance I value. All have made my vision a reality!

Introduction

Neurons. Axons. Serotonin. Synapses. Dendrites. How do these have any application to my daily interactions with young children? How do I use the knowledge gained by brain research to improve my teaching? Many knowledgeable providers in the early care and education field are pondering these questions. It is important for parents and teachers to know the biology that surrounds learning so they can evaluate the environment and make changes to improve the potential success of children. This is called *brain-compatible learning* and means you apply the lessons learned from brain research to plan and create an optimal atmosphere for learning (Gregory and Parry 2006).

Brain research confirms much of what educators have been espousing for years: that the early years are the important years for learning. These beliefs have long been held; now science has validated them:

- Every situation is a learning experience.

- Children need to be nurtured and have physical contact with other people.

- Children learn through their interactions with people and the environment.

- Play is an essential component to learning.

- Hands-on activities result in lifelong learned skills.

- When a child has a choice in selecting her own activities, involvement is increased.

- All children's senses need to be stimulated—though not at the same time—in an enriched atmosphere.

- Activities presented to children should match their stage of development and their interest level.

- Activities that develop the physical, social, emotional, and intellectual aspects of each child are the most effective.

- There should be a balance between activity and rest: between quiet learning and active learning.

- Children need a loving, stress-free environment for optimal learning to occur.

Young children do not learn in a vacuum. Every moment has opportunities for learning, and the environment surrounding the child affects what is learned and how. What educators knew to be best practices has been confirmed in the last twenty years through scientific exploration of how a child's brain operates. From the moment of conception to birth and through the early years of life, the brain is evolving to create new connections based on what children are learning. And learning creates a brain that is more equipped to learn!

Just as a leaky faucet drips to fill a pan or sink, a steady stream of information flows from the child's surroundings, is transmitted to the brain through the child's senses, and builds and builds—leading to learning. This stream of information eventually pours into the river of existing information. This river of information eventually pours into an ocean of knowledge. But reading, writing, and arithmetic are not the only lessons that children learn; they also learn the essentials of human society: to communicate and get along with others in a socially acceptable way, to be motivated to learn and have good self-esteem, and to learn academic subjects and to apply the knowledge to their lives. They learn how to move in space and to apply the principles of investigation and processes to relate one idea to another. Children's development depends on their inheritance of genes plus their interactions within their surroundings. Learning begins the moment children are born and continues throughout life. You are there to guide, help, and move the child from one stage to the next.

ABOUT BRAIN RESEARCH

It is important to remember that brain research is a relatively new science frontier, and that scientific information about the brain changes rapidly. What is discovered today may be updated with new breakthroughs tomorrow. Twenty years ago, researchers understood that babies are born with 100 million brain cells and would never manufacture more.

Today there is growing evidence that brain cells are created under certain circumstances; for example, some mothers experience brain growth in the first months after giving birth (Sohn 2010). Some of the original reports equated all brain cells and neurons with each other. Now we know that *glial cells*, or "glue" cells, keep the environment of the brain free from waste and bring nutrients to each neuron or brain cell. Glial cells make up about 90 percent of the brain's mass. Neurobiologists have begun to understand glial cells' role in growth and development of the brain.

Brain cells called *mirror neurons* have recently been identified. Mirror neurons help young children—and all people—mimic the actions of others. When we see someone yawn, we feel the urge to yawn. This effect might suggest that mirror neurons are at work. Newborns will copy a tongue thrust; small children watch adults and copy their reactions to events. This imitation of a seen behavior, again, may be evidence of mirror neuron activity. Most people smile when seeing someone else smile. Mirror neurons play a major role in each person's ability to empathize and socialize. People depend on others' facial expressions as interactions occur (Society for Neuroscience 2008).

A new scientific field called *fetal origins* is bringing new information to light about the time between conception and birth. We know that smoking, alcohol, poor nutrition, and certain drugs affect the newborn's brain and physical development. We also are learning about the effects of maternal depression and traumatic events—such as war, death of a spouse, poverty, or terrorist attacks, among other things—on the developing fetus. Newborns whose mothers experienced depression or traumatic events while pregnant may have higher levels of stress hormones in their blood. Their babies are more likely to be fussier, harder to soothe, and have sleep problems. As they grow, these children are more disposed to be impulsive, are more hyperactive, and demonstrate emotional and behavioral problems. In addition, longitudinal research shows that negative fetal environments can lead to adults who suffer from mental illness, heart problems, and diabetes (Paul 2010).

Toxic Stress

New science exploration has shown that children who are in neglectful, abusive, or harmful environments (children who do not have secure attachments to their caregivers) exhibit *toxic stress*. Toxic stress is when the body senses a threat and remains at a high level of vigilance for prolonged periods to protect itself. This high level of vigilance means the child's brain floods with chemicals, his heart rate speeds up, and his muscles grow tense; all the systems of the young child's body stay activated and on alert for weeks and months. Toxic stress affects brain development, the wiring of the brain, immunity, and the ability to learn, as well as the emotional and social well-being of the child. Children need to feel safe to grow up healthy in both body and mind. Quality adult-child interactions in a quality child care environment can help ameliorate stress and meet the social and emotional needs of children. A caring, nurturing adult can help relieve out-of-control bodily reactions. Adults can help children deal with adversity and become

resilient. Early care and education personnel have the advantage of their relationships with families. You can direct families to resources such as screenings, assessments, and protective services. Early intervention with professionals can protect children from the stresses in their lives (AAP 2011a).

The scientific exploration of the brain is dynamic and ongoing as new instruments are developed to watch the brain as it functions and learns. The best way to keep current about new brain research is to belong to a professional early childhood association. Such associations keep members informed through bulletins, research journals, position statements, and online resources. Furthermore, the Internet provides reviews of current findings in articles and scientific journals, and television programs often focus on new findings and suggest books and programs or videos. Caution, however, has to be exercised. Many people who don't understand how infants, toddlers, and young children learn give advice on how to apply the research. Products that are purportedly based on current brain theory pop up in the market, but some of these products can be harmful. Stay informed. Talk to coworkers and colleagues and share information. Attend local, state, and national conferences and workshops geared toward parents and teachers of young children. These resources can give you practical tips and help you learn how to revise your curriculum and try new ideas. Also, use common sense about what is good for young children. Teaching now includes a better understanding of how children learn, but what we have known for years about best practices and how adults should relate to young children is still valid. Check out the information thoroughly before drastically changing your practice. Once you are sure of the advantages, try the new technique and decide if it makes a difference for the children in your care.

DEVELOPMENTALLY APPROPRIATE PRACTICE

It is important for early care providers to ensure that everything is appropriate to the child's age and stage of development. The media promotes bombarding young children with flash cards and videos or pushing academics because young brains are developing quickly. Ads for products that claim to teach a baby to read or that show two- and three-year-old children naming all the capitals of every state in alphabetical order or the chronology of US presidents look impressive; but this is an inappropriate use of the research.

Young children can mimic and repeat back almost anything when enough time is devoted to teaching it. Yet the material has never really been learned and is quickly forgotten without daily repetition and reinforcement, especially if meaning is not connected to the memorized material (Sousa 2006, 2008). In essence, it is a waste of the adult's time and the child's effort. We must be diligent in not pressuring young children to memorize facts. Young children need to learn with their senses, through hands-on play. Rote memorization of lists is of little value because children forget the information quickly. This practice can also be harmful if

it creates inappropriate and stressful expectations for children.

Likewise, claims of foods fortified with unproven additives to increase brainpower have little validity. This is a sales gimmick. We have to be intelligent consumers and not believe every pitch to fortify, speed up, or increase brain development.

Setting up an enriching learning environment and intentionally guiding children's interactions with objects brings about learning. Children succeed when they have quality relationships with an adult and a developmentally appropriate curriculum. Knowing the influence that careful planning, a thoughtful curriculum, and enriching activities can have on the outcome of each child is exciting. Early care and education professionals and families do make a difference in the lives of children each and every day!

HOW THIS BOOK CAME TO BE

The Carnegie Corporation of New York had a task force that published *Starting Points: Meeting the Needs of Our Youngest Children* (Carnegie Task Force on Meeting the Needs of Young Children 1994). A grant provided training in the new science of brain research for a small group of early childhood educators. I was fortunate to be selected to learn about the research and was tasked with traveling around the state of Florida spreading information about the results of the research to early childhood providers. After each workshop, teachers would tell me they understood brain biology but couldn't see how that would help their daily teaching. So I began researching books, videos, and articles looking for directions on how to apply this new information. I found nothing.

During this time, Dr. Bernard Maria, who was at the McKnight Brain Institute at the University of Florida, and I served together on an advisory council on early care and education. Together we decided that both early childhood providers and parents needed this information on how children learn. We envisioned a "brain bag" with all kinds of information in different formats at different

educational levels that could become a library of information on the brain. I received a small grant to write and publish the book, giving adults activities that they could easily replicate in their homes and schools to help utilize and apply the brain research. Part of the money was used to develop and distribute the brain bag.

Running an accredited preschool with a quality educational component presented in a developmentally appropriate manner lent itself to the creation of the book. Every activity in the book had been part of the curriculum. The words flowed, the ideas coalesced, and in 2000 the book was written. After it was published by the Early Childhood Association of Florida (later called the Florida Association for the Education of Young Children), I began doing workshops to show teachers and parents how this knowledge could help them teach children more effectively. I believe I have made a difference in how children are taught today. The book you are now reading has been revised and updated to incorporate the latest findings.

HOW TO USE THIS BOOK

This book was written to include the most current brain research on infants, toddlers, and preschoolers and to offer multiple ideas and suggestions on the best environments and appropriate activities needed for a child's brain to grow to its full capacity. If you truly use a developmentally appropriate curriculum and if you are a nurturing person, you most likely already meet the children's needs. You will probably find that you needn't change many aspects of the existing environment to bring the benefits of brain biology studies into your early care and education setting. It is important, however, that you recognize the need to apply the information from the latest brain research to make your teaching the best it can be.

This book contains a description of interest areas in the child's surroundings and includes over six hundred ideas to help you understand the application of brain research in planning activities. Some of the suggestions describe one activity to use

for a day or two. Some of the ideas, such as talking to toddlers about what they are doing, are meant to be practiced every day. Use this book as a reference guide. After writing your weekly lesson plans, assess whether you have activities that engage all the senses and reach all areas of potential growth. Determine which interest areas need more focus and choose an activity that will enhance the children's learning while playing.

This book was designed to be used by classroom teachers, family child care providers, and any person who is involved with young children, includ-

ing parents and families—please invite them to use the book, too. The ideas have been collected over the years from educational colleagues, early childhood conferences, books, and articles, and they represent best practices. All have been successfully used with young children. If you are new to the field, this book will give you a multitude of ideas to expand children's learning. If you have a great deal of experience, the book will reinforce what you already know and perhaps remind you of forgotten extensions. You will enjoy using these activities in children's environments.

CHAPTER 1

Brain Development

Do you remember biology class in high school or college? It was a requirement, and most students memorized facts but didn't necessarily choose it as their favorite class. Now, however, because you are involved in the lives of young children, you are going to change your mind. The biology of the human brain is fascinating! When you read how the brain develops and what you can do to ensure that the growing child is benefiting from this new scientific information, you will find yourself seeking more information in books, magazines, and articles. Don't get bogged down in the scientific words. Instead, go deeper into how to apply this information. You will realize that with this knowledge, you can truly make a difference in children's lives every day.

Effective teachers have long understood how children learn, but they had no way to prove their ideas were valid. The new brain research shows that the early years are the learning years. Science can now demonstrate how experiences drive brain growth. Brain research can indicate what children need from birth to grow and develop to reach their full potential. The information is being used to inform not only educators but also parents, families, legislators, and communities about the importance of investing in young children. Education does not start at the front door of the school. Instead, it is embedded in the daily lives of infants, toddlers, and preschoolers. Brain biology confirms how very young children learn.

BIOLOGY OF BRAIN DEVELOPMENT

Using PET (positron emission tomography) scans and MRI (magnetic resonance imaging), scientists can actually watch as the human brain processes outside stimuli. They can see how a child's brain grows and develops. They can show that a child's environment, with its positive or negative experiences, can affect brain growth and development.

During prenatal stages, the brain develops extremely rapidly, creating 250,000 brain cells per minute. At birth, a full-term baby has around 100 billion brain cells! Most of the cells are *glial*, or "glue" cells, which are the worker ants of the brain. They bring nourishment to the brain cells and remove toxins. The rest are *neurons* or nerve cells. Neurons are the body's most important cells that make up and control the nerve circuitry of the body. They are cells found in the brain that control body functions, memories, and learning (Zero to Three 2011).

Before birth, connections between the neurons begin to develop. Each neuron has the ability to emit electrical impulses and chemicals. Pretend your outstretched arm is the neuron. At one end are the fingers, or dendrites. *Dendrites* are multiple extensions of the neuron with branches that receive electrical impulses and chemicals that are called *neurotransmitters.* A long tube or *axon* (or in this analogy, your arm) transmits the chemicals and electrical impulses to the *axon terminal*, one of which is represented by your shoulder. The axon terminal sends out multiple chemicals and electrical impulses to other neurons' dendrites. The dendrites have *receptors* that receive the emissions. These connections to other neurons are called *wiring*. The neurons do not touch but communicate through tiny spaces called *synapses*. Each neuron can connect to as many as 250,000 other neurons or nerve cells. *Electrochemical messages* move between the neurons at a very rapid pace, communicating what is in the environment. The senses (hearing, seeing, tasting, feeling, and smelling) give input to the neurons through general or specialized sensory receptors. For example, when your eye sees an object, many neurons work together to bring you the visual image.

The developing brain in a fetus establishes neural networks for important life functions such as breathing, a heartbeat, blood pressure and circulation, and digestion so that they are all complete by the time a full-term baby is born. These neural connections are formed in the brain stem at the base of the skull and are connected to the spinal cord. Neural connections from the brain stem extend throughout the brain. Full-term babies have bodies fully functional to sustain life, and their brains are ready for outside input.

Before birth and during the first three years of life, the axon becomes covered with *myelin*, a fatty insulation that protects the neuron like a soft blanket surrounding the long body of the axon. The myelin helps the electrochemical transmitters and electrical impulses flow from one end of the axon to the other. It also protects the neuron so that when the head jerks, the neuron is cushioned. The rapidly expanding density of neuron connections triple the size of the brain until, at age three, the size of the child's brain is about 80 percent of an adult's brain.

Many neuroscientists (Chugani et al. 2001; Perry 2006) have shown that early experiences affect

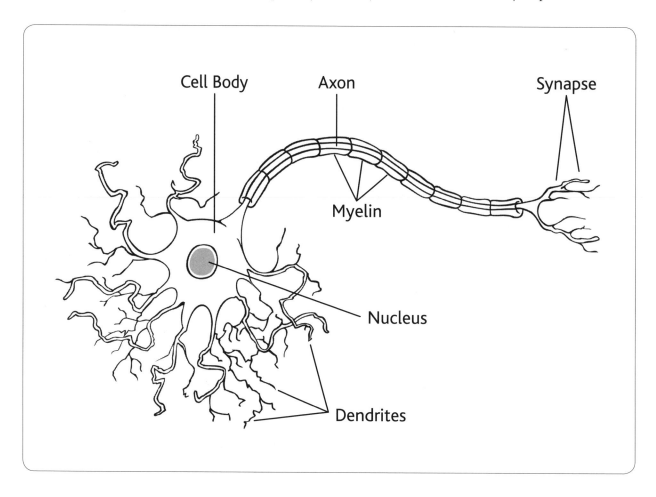

the size of the brain and the number of synapses or connections between neurons. Abuse, neglect, and stress as well as poor nutrition can result in a smaller brain with less capacity to learn. The *limbic system*, which is in the midbrain, controls emotions. It grows disproportionately large in children with prolonged neglect or abuse. These children become hypervigilant, and when they see something they perceive as threatening, their brains emit chemicals that make them want to run away or attack, commonly known as the fight-or-flight response. Physical abuse causes the brain to emit excess neurotransmitters (chemicals) that cause the brain to develop differently, leading to lifelong behavioral and emotional problems (Perry 2006, 2011). Dr. Bruce Perry studied children who lived under extreme stress in the Branch Davidian compounds, and Dr. Harry Chugani and others studied the brains of neglected Romanian orphans. They found that many of these children's brains grew differently than the brains of average well-cared-for children.

Neuroplasticity is the brain's ability to reorganize neural pathways. Connections migrate to different portions of the brain, and the brain prunes, or eliminates, synapses or connections that are no longer needed. Synaptic pruning eliminates weak connections and keeps those that are frequently activated—this is the brain's learning process. Environmental experience determines which connections will be strengthened and which will be pruned. The pruning of synapses makes room for new brain connections to be made. This process occurs throughout our lifetimes as we continue to learn and adapt to new experiences.

It is important to understand brain biology in order to create a stress-free atmosphere that is enriching and challenging, one where young children can learn. In this type of environment, the child participates in meaningful experiences called *brain-compatible learning*. A brain-compatible teacher is aware of the stage of development of each child and understands the child's needs based on that child's brain development. The teacher then meets those needs daily (Gregory and Parry 2006). For example, a teacher should not expect an eighteen-month-old child to cut out a preprinted picture of a train. Instead, the child should be given safety scissors and taught how to use them and then given time to practice snipping strips of paper into small pieces. In this way, the child can be successful and safely try the new activity.

TERMS USED IN BRAIN RESEARCH STUDIES

More than one hundred years ago, Maria Montessori observed children who were preoccupied with learning certain skills. For example, young children would practice standing from a sitting position over and over until they mastered this skill. Children would grasp tiny objects and put them into a container again and again until they had the motor knowledge to do the grasping and releasing of the object without purposeful thinking. These are examples of basic learning, which helps build and strengthen pathways in the brain.

In this context, the phrase *use it or lose it* means that neurons that are used will be maintained, but neurons that are not used will be pruned away. This process can be especially important for the development of senses, such as sight and hearing. Environmental stimuli are important for the formation

Shaken Baby Syndrome

An infant brain is more delicate than an adult brain because it has not yet fully developed. Shaken baby syndrome results when a baby is shaken and the brain bounces against the skull. Symptoms resulting from violent shaking include irritability, lethargy, tremors, vomiting, seizures, coma, stupor, and death. These neurological changes are due to destruction of brain cells from the trauma, lack of oxygen to the brain cells, and swelling of the brain. Extensive retinal hemorrhages in one or both eyes are found in the majority of these cases. Babies should never be tossed in the air and caught as a way to make them laugh. They should never be shaken to make them stop crying. Suspected cases of shaken baby syndrome should be reported, and the baby should be taken to the emergency room immediately!

brain builds internal connections in a network throughout its physical structure to bring about learning, language, memory, physical movements, and other critical functions. In the beginning, the connections are tentative, but as the circuits are used over and over, they become solidified.

MAKING SENSE OF THE WIRING OF THE BRAIN

One conceptual way to look at brain development is to visualize how a grassy field becomes a dirt playing area. When a child is first offered a ball as an emerging toddler, he tentatively pushes it at random. With practice, he can roll it between himself and another person. If that child rolled the ball outdoors in the same exact area, after five minutes or so of the ball going back and forth, the grass would be bent. If the child repeated the rolling exercise over and over, day after day, for a year in the same area, the grass would begin to disappear and a little path would emerge. As the child grows and begins kicking the ball as well as rolling it, the ball would go back and forth on that little path, wearing away at the ground until all the grass had gradually disappeared and only dirt remained. And so the child begins to kick and run with the ball, bounce the ball, catch the ball, use a hockey stick to slam the ball, hit a baseball and run bases, throw and dribble a basketball, and continue to play different ball games in the same area. Over time, the path disappears and the area widens and thickens and all the grass disappears.

of brain connections. For example, fish born in a dark cave have functional eyes, but the necessary connections to their brains for sight never form because they were not exposed to light during their development. Children born with cataracts must have them removed as soon as possible to preserve their capacity for typical vision. The sooner the cataracts are removed, the sooner stimuli can be transmitted to the brain cells so vision can be properly wired.

Much of the new research refers to the *wiring of the brain*. Developing brain pathways has been compared to wiring a home for telephone service. When the home is built, wires are run throughout the walls to each room. The infrastructure is there, but without connecting the wires to the poles outside the home, there is no landline telephone service. This is similar to the state of a child's brain at birth. It is ready to learn and receive messages, but it must be connected, or wired, through stimulation in the environment. If telephone lines are run into only one central receiving station—as in the early 1900s—phone service is limited and must be controlled by an operator. Only when phone lines were connected from city to city, then to continents, and finally through cellular towers, underwater cables, and satellites around the entire world was the communication network complete. Likewise, the child's

The creation of this play area is much like the connections made in a child's brain. Through continuous stimulation to the same area of the brain from repetition and reinforcement, the tentative connections strengthen and become more permanent. Now, if the child moved away and never played in that once grassy area, soon weeds would encroach, grass would reappear, and eventually the path would be hard to find or would disappear completely. This also happens to the brain. Without the repeated stimulation, some connections weaken or disappear. Imagine, however, that the child grows,

matures, and continues playing ball in that area and the parents put down asphalt to create a permanent playing field. They might add a basketball hoop, paint lines for bases, add a tetherball and a football or hockey goal. Even when the child moves away, the area remains viable—and the grown child can use it again without relearning the games. When tasks are repeated frequently until they are mastered, the wiring in the brain in an area becomes strengthened. Eventually the connections become durable and will be a more permanent part of the adult's brain functioning.

Another phrase used is *window of opportunity* or *sensitive period*. Psychologists Jean Piaget, Sigmund Freud, and Erik Erikson observed times during early life when children were normally able to learn tasks and called them *stages*. Scientific research has confirmed that these are periods in a child's development when the child's brain is the most capable of learning certain skills, known as sensitive periods. The wiring of the brain takes place rapidly as the stimulation the child is receiving promotes the growth of connections between neurons in the brain.

These windows of opportunity for development vary from child to child. The brain is very plastic in young children. Although there are opportune times for skills to be developed, there are circumstances when children make phenomenal strides

after the so-called window has closed. Exposure to a rich environment and a nurturing atmosphere with proper intervention can make a difference in how the brain develops—recovery is possible! However, the learning might be more difficult and may take longer to master after the window has closed.

Brain biology and *neurobiology* are terms used to label the current research being conducted to unlock the secrets of brain function. There are over fifty neurotransmitters, or chemicals, secreted by the brain that affect the formation and function of the neurons or brain cells. *Serotonin, dopamine,* and *norepinephrine* are the names of just a few of these chemicals. Some of the neurotransmitters excite, while others calm the system—there's more about this in chapter 3. The brain's physical structure consists of two halves, or *hemispheres*, which are connected by a structure called the *corpus callosum.* The corpus callosum is made up of white matter, which is the myelin that surrounds the axons of neurons (mentioned earlier in this chapter). Optimum experiences activate the cells in both hemispheres and help them work in concert. Activities that call for children to cross their arms and legs past the midline strengthen the connection between the hemispheres. Each side has regions that control specific functions such as breathing, crying, language acquisition, speaking, and—in fact—everything we do.

Human development depends on both the genetic makeup of a child (nature) and the environment in

which the child lives (nurture). Stimulation of their senses, nutrition, and the quality of care directly affect children's physical growth, their ability to learn, and their emotional makeup. Every moment directly influences how a child's brain is wired. Most of the important neural pathways for motor skills, vision, social and cognitive development, language, and emotion are formed during the first three years of life. That said, the brain's incredible plasticity allows for recovery and success—all children in your care deserve rich environments and supportive adults to help them grow and learn.

Now that you have an overview of how the brain works, let's look at how to apply this information to young children's daily routine. It is not difficult, but as you interact with infants, toddlers, and preschoolers, keep the brain science at the forefront to guide your decisions on what children need to use their brainpower to learn. In this book you will read not only how children learn and retain information but also a variety of ways to introduce them to information that will help them move forward on the continuum that leads to competence.

chapter 2

Development of the Senses

Humans learn through their senses. The senses bring external information about the surrounding physical environment to the brain. External stimuli are received and conducted by sensory receptors in the eyes, the ears, the nose, the skin, and the tongue and are transmitted to the brain. The stimulation from the senses causes the wiring of the brain to take place. The senses are:

- Hearing

- Seeing

- Touching

- Tasting

- Smelling

- Kinesthetic sense
  (moving and
  balancing)

DEVELOPMENT OF THE SENSES: THE INFANT AND TODDLER YEARS

HOW SENSES DEVELOP IN INFANTS AND TODDLERS

Before birth, the brain makes connections from the receptors in the eyes, nose, mouth, skin, and ears to specific areas in the brain designated for sight, smell, taste, touch, and sound. This process continues after birth, when sensory exposure dramatically increases. Repeated stimulation helps the infant learn; that is, it helps the infant form a series of connections between neurons in different parts of the brain. Right after birth, infants will respond to loud sounds with a startle reflex. If they hear the same sound over and over in the environment over a period of time, they learn to either ignore the noise or respond appropriately to the sound. Newborns will turn their heads toward a person talking. Mirror neurons fire when infants see someone perform a movement, such as a tongue thrust (sticking out the tongue) or smiling, and this can cause neurons to release electrical impulses—this release is known as *firing*—and the infant will make the same movement. Mirror neurons fire not only for movement but for feelings as well. When infants see an expression of feelings, their neurons for those feelings also are fired. Said another way, when a young child sees someone who is scared or crying, the child may express and experience similar feelings (Iacoboni 2008). This may lead to empathy for others (Carew, Goldberg, and Marder 2008).

Children use all the senses together to interact with their environment and to gain control of their bodies. When a child sees a ball, she sees the color and the shape and feels the surface texture. She hears her caregiver ask if she wants the ball. She reaches out with the appropriate hand and balances her body as she tries to grab it. She feels the smooth, cool surface of the ball. She brings it up to her mouth to taste it and to feel the texture with her lips and tongue. She smells the fabric. All the senses work together in order for the child to experience "ball."

Developing the refined use of the senses requires more than just brain wiring working in concert. Children have to learn how to interpret the input from the senses. The ability to use our senses develops during the early years. Experience teaches us about the sensory input. Children need a multitude of activities that engage their senses if they are to understand the stimuli around them. When deaf adults have a cochlear implant and can hear for the first time, they must learn how to listen and to interpret the signals their brains are suddenly experiencing. Just like all other areas of learning, the environment for young children has to allow them to explore and learn from their senses.

Hearing

The sense of hearing is refined very rapidly, and its circuitry is complete in the first few months. Just as with smells, infants learn to recognize familiar voices and are soothed by them. They enjoy toys that make noise or music, and are fascinated with the sounds of their own voices. As early as two months of age, infants start babbling. Then they refine this repetition of vowels and consonants to repeat the sounds heard in the language spoken in their proximity. Infants respond to higher frequencies; thus it is important to talk to infants using *infant-directed speech*, commonly known as parentese (or motherese or caregiverese), a singsong, higher-pitched speech that attracts young children. To learn language, it's not enough for you to just talk nonstop in a singsong voice; young children need to hear *task-centered talking* accompanied with appropriate facial expressions and gestures or pointing. Task-centered talking, a term coined by David Sousa (1998), is a running narration about what the child is doing or what is being done for them (feeding, dressing, or bathing). It helps young children hear the rhythm and cadence of language as well as exposes them to vocabulary and syntax. It describes what children see and what is happening in their environment. It helps connect meaning to what is happening around them (Sousa 2006). Hearing is a sense crucial for spoken language acquisition. Children's hearing should be checked periodically by a physician, especially if their language skills do not meet developmental milestones.

INFANT & TODDLER ACTIVITIES

Support Hearing

❯ Use words and simple sentences to describe what infants and toddlers are doing and to describe what you are doing with them, whether diapering, dressing, or taking a walk. Your voice patterns will establish a beginning for understanding language. Use task-centered talking.

❯ Use a singsong and higher-pitched voice to hold infants' attention and help them learn language. Sometimes talk normally and sometimes whisper to let infants hear the difference in volume, speed, and pitch of language.

❯ Echo infants' and toddlers' verbalizations back to them to help them learn. Infants babble the vowels and later the consonants of the language spoken

around them. Echoing reinforces their attempts at verbalization.

❯ Play music that is restful before naptime and livelier during playtime, but don't have music on all the time. Infants can block out continuous music, much as adults stop hearing background music. Music boxes offer a pleasant sound as infants look at mobiles or a baby gym.

❯ Sing to infants often. Sing using a high voice, then repeat using a normal or low voice. Don't worry if you can't carry a tune. Infants will love the sound.

❯ Use nursery rhymes to let infants and toddlers hear the cadence and rhythm of rhyming words. Exaggerate and vary voice pitch in reciting nursery rhymes.

❯ Have a variety of rattles, balls, and toys that make a noise when they move. This encourages the child to shake, roll, or pull to hear the noise.

❯ Many toddlers enjoy a jack-in-the-box and respond to both the sound of the music box and the sound as the box opens and the clown pops out. Windup toys often make sounds.

❯ When you hear environmental sounds like a fan, thunder, or the washing machine, mimic the sound, and explain what it is. Encourage older infants and toddlers to repeat the sound. As you read books or play with toys, incorporate sounds such as a duck quacking or a car rumbling.

Seeing

At birth, infants can see only things that are about eight to twelve inches away from their face, just the right distance for them to see the face of the person holding them. And even then, that face is blurry! Their eyes are receiving visual information, but their brains have not yet developed the receptors needed to see clearly. Their eyes develop rapidly, and soon they learn to identify caregivers by sight. After a few months, infants can follow moving objects and turn and look when they hear a sound. They can see objects that are farther away, see the differences in colors, and begin to acquire depth perception. Later in infancy, interacting with brightly colored toys helps develop their network of synapses or brain connections. This skill refinement continues until about six months, when the brain connections are complete and infants' vision is about 20/25 (Heiting 2010). From this point, infants are working on hand-eye coordination and judging distance to objects. Physicians know that eye problems, such as congenital cataracts, extreme nearsighted or farsighted vision, or eyes that turn outward or inward, need to be dealt with as early as possible. Correcting eye complications early allows the connections between the eyes and the brain to develop.

INFANT & TODDLER ACTIVITIES

Support Seeing

❯ Describe what the infant sees. Simple one- or two-word descriptions are sufficient for a young child. As the toddler begins to point, identify what he is pointing to, first using one or two words and then again in a short sentence: "Ball. You see a big ball." As the child matures, increase the length of the description.

❯ Keep a pleasant, animated face to give infants and toddlers a feeling of security.

❯ Provide colorful posters or pictures placed at eye level. Describe what the child sees. Be careful not to overwhelm infants and toddlers with too much visual stimulation.

❯ Read books and other printed material to children right from birth. Make it a time for cuddling and lap sitting to help instill a love of reading. If the story is long, keep it short and simple by "reading" the pictures as you point to them rather than the written words. Add gestures, such as pretend eating or smelling a flower. Older infants will imitate the motions, building a better understanding of what they see.

Smelling

Infants have a heightened sense of smell and taste. In the beginning, infants identify people through sound and smell. They respond to the smell of their mother and her milk and root for the breast. They identify a comfort toy or blanket by its smell. Sometimes adults try to replace a comfort object with another toy or blanket that looks exactly the same. Infants can tell the difference in the smell and often will not accept the replacement article.

INFANT & TODDLER ACTIVITIES

Support Smelling

❯ Provide familiar-smelling blankets or toys when a child is upset; the familiar smell may provide comfort.

❯ Speak of odors using descriptive words to help children learn smells. Identify the smell of different foods, a dirty diaper, or fresh-cut grass.

❯ Demonstrate to older infants and toddlers how to sniff at a flower or a piece of fruit. Encourage them to imitate you. Describe the smell.

- Read sniff-and-smell board books. As they get older, provide scented markers. Just be careful they are nontoxic and don't go into mouths.

- When out for a walk, take time to let toddlers hold and smell new items, so long as the item is safe. If you pass a bakery or other business emitting a smell, use descriptive words such as "sweet," "sharp," and "icky" as you talk about the smells.

- Add lavender and other soothing aromas to hand-washing or bathwater to help infants and toddlers relax.

Tasting

Infants use taste to learn about their world. They have more sensory receptors in their mouths and on their tongues than anyplace else on their body. A very young child mouths a doll with her tongue and lips, tasting the skin and hair, feeling the smooth plastic of the skin in contrast to the rough strands of the hair or the terrycloth body. It is difficult to separate what an infant tastes and what an infant feels when an object goes into her mouth. Since everything goes into the child's mouth for exploration, it is important to make sure all toys are too large to be swallowed and don't have any loose parts.

Taste is intertwined with young children's nutrition. Infants who are breast-fed often refuse formula. As they grow and are introduced to new foods, the taste buds take on a new role. It often takes patience to help a child learn to eat new foods—sometimes a new food needs to be offered ten times before a child will like it!

INFANT & TODDLER ACTIVITIES

Support Tasting

- Make sure everything within reach is clean and sanitized, as infants put everything into their mouths.

- Describe and comment on the taste when new foods are introduced. Continue offering the same food for a while, so children can become familiar with the taste of that food. Make interesting comments that describe the texture they are feeling plus the sweet, salty, or sour taste.

- Connect the temperature of different foods with the taste. Soon very young children will learn about cool, cold, warm, and hot.

Touching

Touch is highly developed at birth. Infants love skin-to-skin contact and respond to patting and hugging. Premature infants are often put into *kangaroo care*, during which they are held skin-to-skin with the mother. Infants are calmed by massage; feel secure when swaddled; and feel love and nurturance when appropriately held, hugged, and touched. These types of touch have positive effects on infants' growth and development and their emotional security. Young children who are not held, cuddled, and hugged may not make the necessary brain connections and may not bond with their caregivers, which can lead to mental health problems at an early age.

As infants mature, they reach out and touch everything in their proximity. They also explore their bodies using this sense. Hands as well as objects go

into their mouths. While being held, infants often stroke the adult holding them. This is an important beginning step of socialization.

Support Touching

❯ Touch infants and toddlers often. In the beginning, take an infant's hands and touch your nose, cheek, fingers, and so on as you name what the infant is touching. Allow young children to explore you by touching your face and hands. Describe the feel of skin to the child.

❯ Help infants explore their own feet and hands. As they put them in their mouths, they will also be experiencing the feel and taste. They explore all kinds of surfaces and experience textures with their tongues.

❯ Provide a variety of objects and textures for them to feel. Use textured blankets, balls, and other commercial products designed for an infant's touch, or collect a mix of textures from around the environment to provide variety. Guide very young children's hands to feel objects as you talk about them. Rub soft blankets on cheeks and arms.

❯ Hold infants and toddlers often. Hug and cuddle them. This behavior demonstrates love and helps with bonding and feelings of security.

❯ Teach infants and toddlers to hold and cradle dolls and stuffed animals. This will give them comfort and help them learn how to give good touches.

❯ Massage infants and toddlers using established infant massage techniques. Explore books and websites devoted to infant massage.

The Kinesthetic Sense

The kinesthetic sense—or knowing where the body is in space, feeling body movement, and maintaining balance—is dependent on touch and sight and comes with experience. Today many infants are carried in car seats and baby carriers or pushed in strollers for convenience. Pick up young children often and hold them close to your body. Personal touch not only helps the child feel secure, it also is important to their growth and development and aids bonding. Infants become aware of their movements and the position of their arms and legs. This sense develops slowly and helps infants reach out to grab toys, roll over, sit up, crawl, stand, and walk.

Support the Kinesthetic Sense

❯ Rock infants and toddlers as you hold them, which is very comforting. Rocking upset children is very soothing.

❯ Provide open space for infants to move. They find pleasure in moving their bodies as they roll over, rock on their knees, or crawl. As infants become mobile, they will enjoy the feel of walking, climbing, and running.

❯ Dance together with music. Be gentle with young children, but help them feel the rhythm as you rock and sway to music. Once they are up and walking, hold toddlers' hands to dance; however, they will still enjoy being picked up to dance.

❯ Allow infants to be in a baby swing for a short time. Take young children to the park and help them gently swing. As they get older, increase the intensity. Add descriptive words to the movement.

❯ Help toddlers balance on one foot as they get dressed. Teach them to hop or jump.

❯ Use steps to help toddlers climb. Make sure you are holding a hand or standing behind them at first to help them climb safely.

DEVELOPMENT OF THE SENSES: THE PRESCHOOL YEARS

HOW SENSES DEVELOP IN PRESCHOOLERS

Perceptual development, or the development of the interpretation of sensorial information (sound, sight, touch, taste, and kinesthesia), doesn't just happen the way that growing taller does. Children have to be able to interpret the signals their eyes, ears, skin, nose, and body bring to them and to use the information. This ability is a kind of intelligence. Like all other knowledge, sense stimuli have to be experienced in a variety of ways to bring meaning to the sensation. Just hearing a noise is not enough. The ear may hear the sound, but unless the brain interprets the information and relates it to something, the sound is meaningless. Understanding a sound comes from knowing its cause or source.

All children should have daily activities that stimulate every sense. Activities for an older child often limit sensory input to seeing and hearing. Yet, only through the interplay of all senses can a child learn to the fullest. The exception to this would

be taste: most older children do not put objects in their mouths to taste them. They rely on their other senses for information about the objects. They mainly use their mouths and tongue to taste, not feel as infants and toddlers do. Often adults must incorporate sensory activities into the preschool environment to ensure that all senses are stimulated every day. Conversations during snack- and mealtimes need to hone in on the taste and texture of foods. Preschoolers can be encouraged to identify smells and textures of their foods. If the stimuli are not naturally in the classroom, bring them in so that the senses aren't neglected. Children will delight in exploring temperatures and textures of foods such as a smooth apple, a cold banana, or a bumpy orange rind with their tongues. Some foods are sticky, some soothing, and others crunchy. Your imagination and creativity can expand on these ideas.

Hearing

Hearing is refined during the preschool years. Listening skills are very important for language acquisition. Vocabulary and enunciation are dependent upon listening. Hearing the phonemes and syllables in words is directly related to the ability to read. Illness and infections affect hearing, so children need to have their hearing checked annually.

PRESCHOOL ACTIVITIES

Support Hearing

❯ Use task-centered talking to describe activities as children go about their daily routine. Use simple sentences for younger children; expand and make the sentences more complex using descriptive vocabulary as children grow.

❯ Use tone and pitch to express feelings.

- Make music an integral part of every day. Sing to boost language acquisition. Singing a simple set of directions lends some fun to learning a necessary bit of information. Give simple directions that are age appropriate to help children be successful in their listening. Start with one direction. When a child can easily follow, add a second direction, then a third. Try to keep the activity positive and fun.

- Provide activities that introduce a variety of sounds. Use words that not only identify the sounds but also are descriptive, such as "loud," "soft," "blasting," and "quiet" to increase both understanding and vocabulary.

- Avoid exposing children to noisy atmospheres for prolonged periods. Some children react to loud noises with out-of-control behavior. Make sure headphones and ear buds do not have loud music blasting into the child's ear. Prolonged exposure results in hearing loss.

- Provide quiet periods as well as times with purposeful listening activities. Quiet can be very relaxing.

- Spark interest with toys that make sounds, such as balls, cars, and trains. Help children mimic the sounds as they play. Listen to instrumental recordings and help children identify and imitate the sound they hear.

- Point out environmental sounds. Help connect the sounds to the object making the noise. Discuss the different pitches and tones they hear.

- Listen to children when they talk. This models listening skills for them.

- Play taped stories and music to hone listening skills.

- Be silly and creative with known nursery rhymes. Change the pitch of your voice and encourage the children to follow as you sing "Itsy Bitsy Spider" and "Great Big Spider" or "I'm a Little Teapot" and "I'm a Great Big Teapot."

Seeing

Even though the circuitry of vision is completed in infancy, visual discrimination continues to develop over time. *Acuity*, or the ability to see not just the object but also the details of the object, improves with age. Children need the ability to distinguish between spaces, lines, and shapes to be able to identify letters. They need to focus on the differences between similar letters like "p" and "b" so they can read the difference between "pear" and "bear." They will have to learn the difference between pastel blue and navy and distinguish between the shape of a seashell and a jellyfish before deciding to pick it up. All these visual clues have to be learned. From age three, children should have their eyes checked periodically. Only through a visual screening can amblyopia, or "lazy eye," be diagnosed. If not treated, the child could lose sight in that eye.

PRESCHOOL ACTIVITIES

Support Seeing

- Describe what children see, both real objects and pictures. Make the descriptions more complex as children grow older.

- Point out colors, objects, and shapes in the surrounding environment. Help children see the variety of what can represent "blue," "hat," or "dog."

- Teach children how to recognize body language and connect it to feelings. Examine faces, arm gestures, and stances. Connect feelings to the movements so they can see the difference between anger and pleasure. Try to keep a cheerful, positive appearance to give them a secure feeling.

- Provide a variety of colorful, culturally diverse posters or pictures placed at eye level to entice and delight children. Show various family configurations and community helpers. Talk about what they see. Give children a descriptive vocabulary linked to what they are seeing. Match the sentence structure to the child's maturity.

- Read books and other printed material often. The more children see print in a meaningful situation, the more they are prepared for reading. Read with a child on your lap or sitting close by. Pleasurable reading activities lead to later enjoyment of reading.

- Vary repeated activities by adding visual surprises. Place colored cellophane over the fish tank or hide colored rocks in the sand table. Add food coloring to water, glue, or homemade playdough.

- Put a drop of washable food coloring inside a home-made playdough ball. The color appears as the child kneads the ball. Place food coloring in a glass of water and add a flower or celery stalk. The color will travel up from the water into the object.

- Provide magnifying glasses for children to examine flowers, leaves, and shells. Let children look through a kaleidoscope. Talk about the differences when looking at an object with and without sunglasses.

- Identify the aroma of different foods as they are cooked and eaten to create knowledge of smells. The senses of smell and taste are closely related.

- Teach children the smell of books as you read or the smell of dirt as you garden, which helps them cement the object's odor into memory.

- Use markers and sniff-and-smell storybooks with scent added. Supervise closely so these do not go into mouths.

- Add activities to the curriculum to foster olfactory knowledge. Add spices to a collage, add a few drops of peppermint extract to the water table, and use naturally scented hand cream after washing hands. Be mindful of children who may be extra sensitive to smells, and do not use artificial fragrances.

- Place a cotton ball with drops of an extract on it in an empty spice bottle with a lid with holes. Glue the lid to the bottle to prevent removal of the scented cotton.

Smelling

Smell is learned in the infant and toddler years but honed in the preschool years. With experience, children can learn to distinguish the smell of a fresh apple and a cooked apple or a musty book and a new book. Descriptive vocabulary helps them to define smells. The goals are to see something and know what it smells like and to label the smells in their immediate vicinity.

Call children's attention to aromas associated with rain, cooking food, or paint. Encourage smelling flowers, leaves, and dirt when outside. Don't ignore environmental smells.

Tasting

Children improve their skill at identifying the taste of foods. With experience tasting a large variety of foods with accompanying descriptive vocabulary, they will be able to look at a food and know its taste. They can identify what they do taste. Getting preschoolers to try new foods is often difficult. They may model the likes and dislikes of others without really tasting the food. Challenge them to try a taste and assure them that as they mature, their tastes should change.

PRESCHOOL ACTIVITIES

Support Smelling

- Take notice with young children of odors in their immediate surroundings. Link odors with descriptive words to help them learn smells. Identify the smell of rain and of fingerpaint.

PRESCHOOL ACTIVITIES

Support Tasting

- Create times during snacks and meals to discuss and compare the taste of foods. This helps make the connections in the brain so children eventually know the taste of a food from seeing it. Describe the foods they are eating.

- Encourage children to experience and taste a variety of foods. It is okay for children to dislike some foods. Use descriptive language to identify the taste: "You like sour foods. Pickles are sour, just like lemons."

- Cook with young children. This is not only fun; it also provides opportunities to distinguish the taste and texture differences of a raw carrot from a cooked carrot. Children enjoy eating foods they prepare. See pages 61–63 and 96 for more about cooking with children.

- Include salty (pretzels), sweet (fruit), sour (pickle), and an occasional bitter (radish) food for children to experience. Keep the activity fun, and never force children to taste new foods.

- Offer a variety of foods from different cultures. Discuss how soy sauce is salty and salsa is spicy.

- Compare the tastes of some of these foods:

  • Sweet and dill pickles or black and green olives

  • Oranges and tangerines, lemons and limes, or pink and white grapefruit

  • Green and wax beans or pinto and black beans

Touching

Preschool children can identify objects by touch alone and thus sharpen their knowledge of the feel of surfaces. This doesn't happen in isolation, but rather in a carefully sequenced interaction with their environment. The more opportunities they have to feel different textures with descriptive vocabulary, the better they will be in discerning differences. Just as you comment on the colors of items in their environment, try also to talk about the feel of something: "This leaf is green and feels smooth, but this brown leaf is scratchy and crumbles easily." "Can you feel the veins in this leaf?" When you show interest in an attribute, the children will be interested too.

Support Touching

❯ Touch and hold preschoolers appropriately and often. Hug and cuddle them and provide lots of lap time. Describe the feel of the child's skin as you rub her face or arm.

❯ Add varied textures to the environment. Smooth and rough materials as well as hard and soft toys teach concepts as the children play with them. Provide plastic, metal, wood, corduroy, velvet, and burlap to compare the textures. Use descriptions to help children move the information into memory.

❯ Provide a feely box so children can identify objects by touch not sight.

❯ Connect words to the surfaces of objects as children touch and feel. Increase descriptive words as children get older. Play matching games based on the textures and shapes of different objects.

❯ Teach young children to touch, hold, and cradle dolls and stuffed animals. These skills will translate into empathy with peers and younger children and later on into parenting skills.

❯ Paint with warm fingerpaint and add ice to the water table for a different experience.

❯ Play with cornstarch dissolved in water to excite the touch modality. Experiment with getting the correct consistency by adding a little water at a time to a box of cornstarch. It can be picked up and then dripped back into the pan. This is fun, and cleanup is easy.

❯ Vary the contents of the water and sand table. Add potting soil and containers to fill. Talk about the difference in the feel of sand and water. On another day, add water to the soil to create mud. Talk about the feel compared to the dry dirt. Place gravel or small rocks for a different feel.

❯ Place rounded pebbles, sand, potting soil, and water in individual tubs that children can walk in. Help children walk barefoot through this maze of textures. This "feely walk" is best done outdoors near a hose to wash off feet.

❯ Help young children learn how to touch other children in a socially acceptable manner. Use songs and games to teach good touches.

The Kinesthetic Sense

Kinesthetic knowledge allows preschoolers to race around the playground, participate in creative movement exercises, and dance. They learn how to balance their bodies and know the positions of their bodies in the surrounding area. Young children find pleasure in moving their bodies and have a difficult time being still. Moving feels good and is enjoyable. As they gain control of their arms, hands, fingers, legs, and feet, they strengthen their understanding of their bodies in space. Give them the freedom to move by eliminating time sitting in chairs or on rugs on the floor. Expect the children to be moving so they feel good about not sitting for long periods. Children often learn best when they can move and interact with both people and objects in their immediate vicinity.

Support the Kinesthetic Sense

❱ Put movement together with music. Add a rhythmic beat to the action. Swaying, hand motions, and creative movement are stimulating to many parts of the brain simultaneously.

❱ Include opportunities that promote balance, such as putting on dress-up clothes and walking on a painted line, a log, or a low balance beam. Play games that have children stand on one foot, put one arm on the floor, and other activities that rely on body balance.

❱ Provide opportunities to swing and slide to help children develop control of their bodies as they move. Hold hands and sway back and forth and side to side.

Move in a circle or spin slowly around. Bend down and jump up. Turn around with arms in the air. Fly like a bird or a plane.

❱ Use creative movement exercises freely. Utilize the many creative movement songs and videos available to help children learn where their bodies are in space.

❱ Teach simple dances. Play lively music, and let the children create their own dance.

❱ Use tumbling mats for somersaults and body rolls. Offer gymnastics and acrobatics on rainy days.

❱ Run with kites or paper plates on a string. Play sports that have children swinging a bat or a golf club, kicking a ball, or running bases.

❱ Challenge children to use their bodies to form letters or numbers.

CLOSING THOUGHTS

Children are born with sensors that send signals to the brain that enable sight, smell, taste, hearing, and a kinesthetic sense of where their body is and what position it is in as it moves. The senses are the only way our brains have to receive outside information. Children must gain experiences with each as well as gain an understanding of how to recognize and use their perceptions. Children accomplish this learning through opportunities that teach them how to interpret the sensations. Sensory input is necessary for physical, emotional, social, and intellectual growth. All of a child's abilities are related to the use of his senses.

When planning an enriching environment, make sure you vary the sensory input offered daily. It is easy just to have children listening to the same music or listening to surrounding talk and naturally occurring environmental sounds. It doesn't take much to provide a variety of colorful toys and books for children to see. It does take time, however, to ensure that sensory offerings are balanced and there are daily opportunities to hear new sounds or variations of known sounds. It does take planning to point out multiple, minute details for children to see, to enhance the smells available, and to discuss a variety of textures and tastes. The effort taken to enhance the sensory environment is well worth it. The reward is children who are constantly engaged in extending their sensory learning and curious about the world around them.

CHAPTER 3

Emotional Development

Throughout our entire lives—even in a single day—people feel a variety of emotions. Children need to learn that it is normal and natural to have these emotions. They also need to learn to master the words that communicate their feelings to people in their environments. Gaining control of emotions is primary to learning. During the first five years of life, children begin to develop *emotional intelligence*, which is the ability to understand and manage emotions and use them appropriately in our society (Goleman 2012). Once in elementary school, children are expected to have mastered their emotions, and little time is spent teaching skills that foster self-confidence and self-esteem. The reality is that a child must know how to regulate and express emotions and, whether at home or school, to interact with others. Knowing how to control and appropriately express one's own emotions is critical to success in everything a child does. The brain has to be wired—through repeated experiences—to allow the child to feel emotions, understand what she is feeling, describe that feeling, and be in command of her actions.

The goal of this chapter is to give adults ways to teach young children about their emotions, to help children understand emotions, and to teach children socially acceptable ways to express their emotions. Learning begins in infancy and is closely tied to the level of care. As young children interact in the world, they find themselves experiencing new emotions. You can begin to teach even infants and toddlers self-control and self-regulation. As they mature, children need to learn how to express the feelings they have and why they feel the ways they do. Children need competence with these skills to interact with people in their families, schools, and communities.

When young children are experiencing strong emotions, adults need to act in a timely and respectful manner—children's emotions are real. When a child is upset or scared, instead of trying to talk the child out of the emotion, validate the feelings, and then help the child move on: "That fall really hurt your leg. I know you want your mommy to help. Come sit on my lap, and I will rub your leg to make it feel better," or "Daddy had to leave, and that makes you feel very sad," or "The dark can be scary. I will hold your hand." Unless children feel loved, safe, and respected, they cannot thrive. Learning can only take place after children's anxieties are relieved. Adults should not only soothe children but also teach them to take charge of their own emotions.

EMOTIONAL DEVELOPMENT: THE INFANT AND TODDLER YEARS

The first eighteen months are crucial to healthy emotional development. It is necessary for infants and toddlers to make an attachment or bond with family members *and* the primary caregiver in a child care setting. This promotes good mental health and enables children to feel safe, which allows them to learn and grow; emotional well-being impacts all areas of a children's development. By eighteen months, children in a nurturing environment with adults they can trust begin to learn how to control their emotions (Brazelton 2006). The brain is on track for healthy development.

The neurons or nerve cells connect to each other through tiny spaces called *synapses*. Chemicals called *neurotransmitters* are released from one neuron across the synapse to be picked up by another neuron. There are many types of neurotransmitters, and they have a wide range of functions to promote communication in the brain. Serotonin, dopamine, and norepinephrine are among the neurotransmitters that are especially important for communicating emotions.

Many other chemicals also affect the developing brain. Cortisol, for example, is a hormone that is released during times of stress. Everybody has some cortisol in their system at all times, but our levels of cortisol change throughout the day. When cortisol levels in the body become too high due to threats from the environment or a chronically stressful situation (such as neglect or maltreatment), the brain and body suffer negative consequences. See the introduction for more information on toxic stress.

PRENATAL AND INFANT STRESS

The stress hormones a pregnant woman experiences may cause her baby to have a lower birth weight, a lag in brain and physical development, and a more sensitive and emotionally reactive infancy. After birth, a chaotic atmosphere or a neglectful environment forces children to adapt by becoming *hyperaroused* (responding very strongly to typical sensory input) or *dissociative* (disengaging from or underresponding to typical sensory input). High levels of cortisol are released during these periods of stress, causing the brain's chemistry to be altered. If violence, neglect, unreliability, and high noise levels characterize a child's primary relationships, the child will have a brain that is not ready for learning (Perry 2011). Early intervention for infants and toddlers can be effective, but it is best to prevent mental health disorders by providing an optimal emotional atmosphere.

THE OPTIMAL EMOTIONAL ATMOSPHERE FOR INFANTS AND TODDLERS

Infant mental health depends on the care and nurturing during the first few months of life. Emotional development is extremely influential on brain development and vice versa. The quality of the nurturing and love a child receives is an important component that influences not only how the brain is wired but also how the brain grows physically. Warm interactions and feelings of trust and safety are necessary for the child to reach optimum growth and development. Children can only thrive in a loving, accepting environment where they feel safe and know their needs are being met.

Providing a format to discuss upset feelings at a time when children are not upset can be advantageous. The goal is for the child to develop an understanding of self and be able to verbalize feelings, understand abilities, and exhibit self-control and self-esteem. Teachers want to help children change behavior as they react to their surroundings.

Tantrums

When very young children are frustrated and don't understand their feelings, they exhibit their distress with a tantrum. They have used all the skills in their arsenal to get what they want, and nothing has worked. Without the language and the resources to get what they want when they want it, children can lose control and have a tantrum. Tantrums can manifest themselves in different ways. Toddlers' tantrums can be long, uninterrupted crying sessions and can involve children throwing themselves on the ground, kicking and screaming. Some children bite themselves or bang their heads. Some children may throw nearby objects or purposely destroy a block tower, completed puzzle, or other object. All tantrums are developmentally normal at this age,

and most children exhibit some form of the behavior during their toddler years. How you react to the tantrum is crucial. Anger should never be a part of the reaction. Patience is paramount. For infants, using a soothing voice and gentle touch often calms the child. Others are inconsolable and don't react to a gentle touch or voice but need to know the caregiver is nearby to support them as they learn to calm themselves. Toddlers' needs are a little different. They, too, need a caring adult nearby; however, when children are so emotionally upset, trying to

soothe them with words and touch doesn't work because they are too focused on being upset. In fact, attempts to distract children from their anger by asking questions or redirecting can cause the tantrum to last longer. The best technique is to ignore the outburst, keep the child within sight to ensure safety, and then be ready to offer comfort when the child has calmed and is receptive to your support.

Knowing what triggers tantrums and intervening before that happens can sometimes prevent tantrums. A routine in the infant's or toddler's daily life provides a sense of security. Therefore, they learn that when they are hungry or tired, their needs will be met. Prepare young children for a routine change. Inform children about what you are doing before you do it, and if possible with toddlers, give them a choice so they feel independent. The choices are yours—but make them real and of consequence for the child. For example, you might say, "It is time to stop playing. I know you want to continue to play, but you have to stop. Do you want to throw the ball two more times before we clean up, or do you want to see if you can roll it all the way across the room to the toy box?" Or you might say, "It is time to sit down and relax. I know you want to run more, but now is the time to stop. You choose. You can sit on a carpet square or on the green chair." Overtired or very hungry children are more likely to have tantrums. Knowing what triggers the tantrum will help with prevention. Prolonged tantrums that escalate in intensity and continue to intensify may need the intervention of an infant/toddler mental health therapist.

INFANT & TODDLER ACTIVITIES

Promote Emotional Development

❯ Respond quickly to infants' cries to let them know they can depend on you to care for them. This is

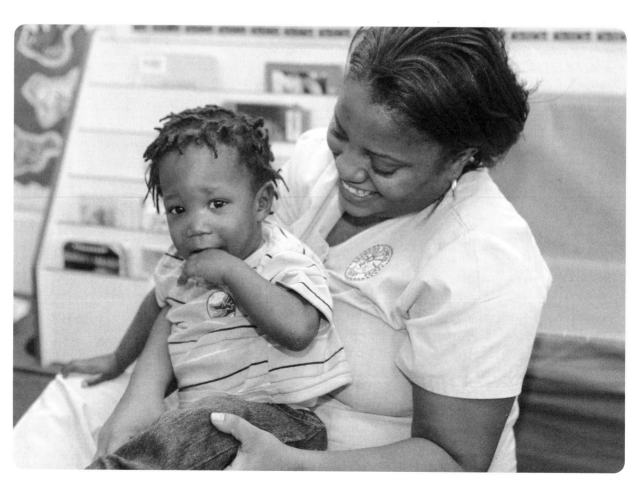

their mode of communication to let you know they are hungry, wet, tired, or uncomfortable.

> Give lots of positive individual attention to infants and toddlers.

> Hold and hug infants and toddlers often. Touch helps all young children develop physically and cognitively.

> Swaddle newborns to help them feel secure.

> Keep noise levels low by using quiet voices.

> Allow infants and toddlers to have their preferred comfort blanket, doll, or favorite object.

> Be a consistent, responsive caregiver at all times.

> Rock young children and hum to them when they are crying or sad, and help calm them by using a soft, soothing voice.

> Sit toddlers on your lap facing you and talk with them about their body parts. Play "Patty-Cake" and other interactive baby games. Give hugs and pats on the back often during the day.

> Read books while making physical contact.

> Keep a pleasant face near the child during diapering. Talk in a soothing voice describing what you are doing. End with a fingerplay, nursery rhyme, or song.

> Blow bubbles on tummies, sing nursery rhymes, and wiggle fingers and toes in a playful manner.

> Give upset infants a warm bath or gently rub a warm washcloth on their skin to help calm them. Toddlers can play in a water table or sink. This activity distracts them, and the water also soothes them.

> Sit in a rocking chair or on a pillow and hug children as you talk in a quiet voice.

> Convey delight in each young child. Smile often.

> React positively when children attempt new skills whether they succeed or fail. Help them feel good about taking risks.

> Use words that let children know you care about and are interested in what they are doing.

> Allow two-year-olds to say "No!" Punishing them triggers power struggles and leads to tantrums.

> Give toddlers real choices in many situations to allow autonomy to develop. They will feel in control and independent, which leads to self-confidence.

EMOTIONAL DEVELOPMENT: THE PRESCHOOL YEARS

During the preschool years, children's emotional needs still remain primary. The environment must be accepting, loving, and stress-free for children's brains to continue to grow optimally. When children are emotionally secure, their brains are open for learning. The chemicals emitted when children are happy actually allow for cognitive development to occur. The architecture of the brain is dependent on the relationships that children have with the people caring for them. Feelings that emerge wire the brain and create positive or negative reactions to stimuli (Shonkoff and Phillips 2000).

No matter how smart or how accomplished four-year-olds are, they should not be treated like elementary school students. Their brains are different, and they need to learn in ways that are appropriate for their own developmental level. Labeling them prekindergarten children does not elevate their needs. Pushing children ahead, seating them in desks, and expecting them to learn using elementary school curricula is damaging to both their motivation to learn and to their self-esteem (Elkind 2001b).

Our most vivid memories are connected to emotions. We more easily remember ideas and information when we use multiple senses to gain the information and are connected to the experience emotionally. The more senses and emotions we associate with a given memory, the stronger are the synapses and the stronger is the memory. Just seeing a picture of a flower is not of as much value for a young child as having a hands-on encounter. If a child sees a flower, picks it, touches the petals, smells the fragrance, and watches the flower die, more connections will form in the brain. If the caring adult makes the experience particularly pleasant, synapses will also form within the limbic system, which is the key to emotional development (Perry 2006). This is why the simple mention of a rose or daffodil in later life may trigger fond memories of planting a garden with a favorite adult or a bouquet given to mark a special event (Maria 2001).

Here are a few more examples of how actions are connected to emotional memories:

- When children smell cookies, they remember the wonderful fun they had baking cookies with a loved grandmother.

- When children see a rainbow, they might remember laughing and the joy they felt as they ran through a sprinkler.

- When children see an angry face, they remember a yelling adult and fear.

It is during the early years that children's basic attitudes toward themselves, learning, and school are established. Good self-esteem is beginning to form. Children in an educational, play-based program that meets their developmental age, social, and emotional development level can succeed. They enjoy the learning experience and feel good about themselves. Hopefully they will have motivation to acquire skills and knowledge throughout their lives (Elkind 2001b).

THE OPTIMAL EMOTIONAL ATMOSPHERE FOR PRESCHOOLERS

Most early care and education settings move children from class to class by age. The children have a new class and teacher every year. Since nurturing and bonding play such an enormous role in early social and emotional development, it may be better for children to have the same caregiver throughout the early years. We know that young children who are in care for a long day need the continuity of the same caregiver. When the staff changes throughout the day, the children are put at a disadvantage.

When children are under stress, they can't learn what you want them to learn because they are focused on how to respond to the stress. Using good classroom management and appropriate guidance techniques—as well as giving children choices and using transition techniques—helps keep children from misbehaving. This makes it easier for you, too! Children need a loving, nurturing atmosphere.

Teaching about Emotions

Children need to have emotional strength and understand emotions inherent in situations. This is what is called *emotional intelligence*. Teaching children to identify how and what they feel, as well as the emotions other people are experiencing is important. Children can then begin to control their own emotions. Young children need to practice the skills they will need when upset. You can add activities to promote the understanding of feelings. You can achieve this by creating activities that mimic emotions and feelings.

Create Teachable Moments

❯ Let children use a thumbs-up sign for things they like and a thumbs-down sign for items they dislike. Show pictures of foods, toys, and animals and ask children to share likes and dislikes: "Janie and Louis like celery, but Tony won't eat celery." "Andy likes vanilla ice cream, but Charlene likes chocolate best."

❯ Let children decide if they like or dislike characters in a familiar story. Use thumbs up and thumbs down as the story is stopped periodically. Allow children to change their minds based on the behavior of the character. Start with books that evoke strong feelings about characters such as the Frog Prince or

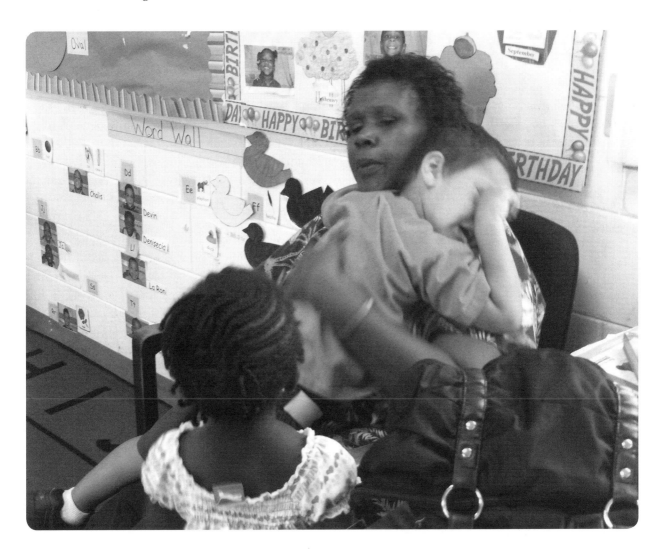

Rapunzel. Once children understand the concept, it is easy to use other books that show a variety of character traits.

> Discuss topics that are upsetting to children: "How do you feel when another child says he hates you?" Reflect their emotions: "It makes you very angry when Darcy says she hates you and you can't come to her birthday party!" "What do you feel when someone won't sit next to you?" "You felt hurt and sad when Willis refused to sit next to you."

> Compare—but don't judge—children's feelings: "Angela gets angry, but it makes Antonio feel sad when a friend tells him he can't join the game."

> Mirror the children's feelings accurately and avoid judgment: "You are very upset that you can't stay outside with the other children."

> Model emotional control and empathy toward others.

> Play games that promote an understanding of body language, such as acting out feelings of loneliness, anger, or joy.

> Look at photographs that depict emotions and help children make up a story about what might have happened to cause the distress or happiness.

> Read books about characters engaged in struggles to enhance children's identification of feelings. *The Little Red Hen*, *Stone Soup*, or *Aesop's Fables* depict success in spite of problems. Read a book or describe an incident that demonstrates joy, distress, or adversity. Use feelings words to describe the emotions the character feels. Stop the story before the conclusion and listen to children's solutions.

> Label both your emotions and those expressed by children when they occur. Empathize with children as they express their emotions.

> Perform a puppet show reenacting an emotional outburst, such as a tantrum or separation problem. Stop the puppet show and ask the children how the puppet could solve the problem. Use their solutions to finish the play. Act out problems and conflict situations. Stop the action before the problem is solved. Help children reach their own conclusions.

> Listen to poetry and music and describe how they make you feel; ask the children how they feel.

> Teach empathy: "Jimmy is upset. What could you say to Jimmy to let him know you didn't mean to knock down his blocks?"

> Play "Follow the Leader" or "Simon Says." Substitute a child's name and let the child lead. Let children take turns leading songs.

Practicing Emotional Skills in Learning Centers

Children find a great deal of comfort in playing with familiar objects in the dramatic play area. Young children enjoy re-creating scenes in their daily lives, such as eating and sleeping. They are fascinated with babies and enjoy playing with dolls and caring for them in much the same way they are cared for by their parents. They want to wear the clothes they see adults wearing.

In reality, children have very little control over their lives. A routine is established and they are made to conform. When the family decides to go out of the house, the child is taken. Meals are served. Children are put to bed. In the pretend area, they suddenly have power, which is personally satisfying. They can practice the daily routine—as they would like to have it—and can re-create difficult situations and learn coping skills. Playing doctor, before or after an illness, helps allay fears. Pretending to be daddy leaving for work and returning strengthens the feeling of trust that an adult will reappear. Re-creating an event at home or taking care of an infant is gratifying. Children learn how to deal with emotions and practice coping skills when engaged in imaginary play. Make-believe allows them to understand frightening events and feel in control. They can act out fears and experience accomplishment through the play experience. The pretend area becomes an outlet for emotions. Children can gain a feeling of mastering their environments. The art and block area lets the child create a project and alter it multiple times. Satisfaction in the outcome brings about positive feelings. The

following is a list of emotional skills children practice while playing in interest centers:

- Focusing

- Understanding and appreciating family dynamics by acting out family roles

- Being independent

- Enhancing self-regulation

- Enhancing self-esteem

- Mastering the environment

- Enjoying learning new facts

- Experiencing a range of emotions

- Feeling successful

- Discovering through trial and error

- Risk-taking

- Delaying gratification until a project is completed

- Acting out feelings in an acceptable way

Support emotional development by making positive statements about what children are doing as they play in interest centers:

- "You are taking good care of your baby. You wrapped your baby in a warm blanket."

- "What a wonderful dad you are! You read a book to your children."

- "What a delicious meal you cooked!"

- "You really dug a deep hole for the plant. You are strong!"

- "You worked hard cleaning the cage."

- "You poured the water carefully and didn't spill a drop."

- "Gluing the sequin on top of the cotton ball makes the cotton ball shiny!"

- "You put the purple in the corner of the paper just where you wanted it."

- "Your circle is very round."

- "This paper is completely covered with paint. You worked very hard."

- "Your tower is nearly as tall as you!"

Separation Problems

The preschool child who cries daily when left in the care of others has an emotional need that must be met. Children have to feel loved, secure, and safe, or else chemicals that make learning difficult are released in the brain. Some children learn to stop the tears because of the threat of punishment or the promise of a treat, but emotionally they are still just as upset. Caregivers must take the time to rock, comfort, and speak to the child until the feelings of sadness go away. If the problem is prolonged, the damage to a child can show up later in life with inappropriate reactions to relationships. Try not to let separation problems go on too long without seeking a remedy. Usually having the parent spend time in the setting with the child helps the upset child work through the fears experienced. Other children need a smaller setting or are not ready to be in a group situation.

Tantrums

Some preschoolers learn during their toddler years that tantrums help them deal with frustration and work to fulfill their wishes. This behavior can be very disruptive, which is part of the reward for the child. In group settings, the reaction of the teacher and the other children contributes to the length and intensity of the out-of-control behavior. Punishment isn't appropriate or effective in stopping tantrums. It might work for the immediate, but it doesn't teach children effective alternatives. Families and teachers need to work together to help children use acceptable ways to express feelings. Many of the techniques that work with infants and toddlers also help preschool children calm themselves.

Since children learn acceptable emotional control through practice and experience, adults need to model and discuss emotions. At a totally separate time, discuss options for the child: "I know you get very upset when you see others playing with your favorite doll. I'd like to help you so you can feel better when other children play with the doll." Then help the child learn that it is okay to be upset, but that there are other avenues to express it. Practice some alternatives with the child. Keep expectations low. You might have to repeat this process multiple times for it to have any effect. Be alert, and when you see an event that will trigger a tantrum, intervene before it happens. Sometimes redirection works; at other times, helping the child express upset feelings in a different way will help. If a tantrum does take place, ignore the anger and

be ready to offer support when the child is calm. Just as with toddlers, if the tantrums escalate and prevent the child from learning, outside intervention from a professional is needed.

Parents and teachers sometimes mistakenly think that if they plead with the child or give in to the child, the tantrum will end. It may for that moment, but the attention becomes a reward for the behavior and the child will repeat it. Some children can exhibit out-of-control behavior for a long time. Waiting until the tantrum has been going awhile and then giving the child what she wants only lengthens the incident. The child learns that if she kicks, screams, stamps her feet, and waves her arms, the adult will give her what she wants. Families and caregivers need to work together to handle tantrums in a united way to help the child learn that tantrums are not acceptable. Then children have to be taught the methods they can use to explain what they want.

PRESCHOOL ACTIVITIES

Calm Children Who Are Upset

❯ Provide art materials and suggest the child draw, paint, or pound clay to help alleviate upset feelings. Suggest the child draw a picture of how he feels (scribbles are acceptable).

❯ Use the words "sad," "angry," and "upset" to give the child a wide vocabulary to express emotions.

❯ Have the child dictate to you the reason for her emotional outburst. Write down word for word what she says, without editing, and read it back to the child. Give the child the paper to hold and carry around. Encourage the child to take the note home to discuss with her family or to post it.

❯ Find a book that will match the emotions the child is expressing. Keep within easy reach books that show characters struggling with various problems.

❯ Provide water play to help calm children.

The Effects of Classroom Stress

Children who participate in an activity-driven classroom have better self-esteem and experience less stress than children who are "taught" in an academic preschool (Elkind 2001b). If adults make impossible demands and challenges for children, or if children are not ready for academics and are pressured to write their names or read before they are developmentally capable, some children may find the experience stressful, which causes their brains to release chemicals that may impair learning. These children may fail and think there is something wrong with them. If enough pressures and demands are made so that children can't succeed, they then begin to dislike themselves and to dislike learning. When the time comes when the child would be capable of accomplishing the task, the child refuses to try (Perry 2003).

Stress can affect learning and memory. Children who feel threatened or very stressed cannot concentrate or participate in activities. The limbic system in the brain, which controls emotions, emits chemicals that direct the child to fight or flee. Some children act out, others withdraw.

PRESCHOOL ACTIVITIES

Provide Stress Busters

❯ Stretching exercises

❯ Deep breathing

❯ Music and singing

❯ Running and jogging

❯ Outdoor free play

❯ Quiet introspection

TELEVISION AND PRESCHOOLERS

Some children's television programs are meant to teach tools to help children cope in their world. Shows such as *Sesame Street, Mister Rogers' Neighborhood,* or *Barney and Friends* focus on important emotional and social issues, such as getting along with other people or the fear of failure. Watching these types of programs with children and helping them discuss issues may be of value. Keep in mind that watching television is a passive activity, and small children need direct experience. Therefore, it's important to always ask yourself if there is a better alternative to watching TV. If the answer is yes, find something else for the children to do.

When children view programs that show people and cartoon characters involved in karate, fistfights, and other acts of aggression, they may become emotionally unsettled. Proponents of these shows argue that the "good guy" perseveres and that there is a moral at the end of each episode. The key word here is "end"—and the lesson is often so brief that young children miss it. They see that the majority of the show is spent in conflict and with a lot of physical action. Because children model behavior they see, they imitate the hero's hitting and kicking. They learn that physical force and aggressive acts are not only acceptable but necessary to win. Viewing such content on television should be eliminated. It does not meet the child's needs in any way and often escalates inappropriate behavior. The more violence they observe, the more accepting and immune children become to violent acts (AACAP 2011). Even though this type of viewing occurs in the home, it is still an issue for preschool teachers. They often see behavior that is fueled by television programs or videos seen in the home. Discussing this with family members is prudent and necessary to help de-escalate aggression.

In addition to being mindful of the content shown in children's programming, it's critical that adults pay attention to what they are watching when children are present. This also occurs in the home, but it affects the child's behavior in the classroom. Children cannot understand news programs showing gunshot victims, earthquakes, and floods. These are incomprehensible occurrences that are difficult for adults to accept. Television shows that focus on war, police, and hospital settings present a view of the world that young children cannot understand. Children are just beginning to process information about death and tragedy. They might begin to worry that what they see on television will happen to them. This apprehension and out-of-control feeling over such situations may trigger a chemical release in the brain that helps children remain vigilant so disaster won't strike. These chemicals can interfere with learning; and the children's fears can affect sleeping and eating. The best solution for providing emotional security is to remove this kind of television viewing from the children's environment.

Young children's attention spans are short. Use television sparingly with young children. Instead, children need active play. Screen time for older children should be limited to one or two hours per day (which includes home exposure) and be coupled with adult interaction (AAP 2011b).

Finding media appropriate for young children takes time, but it pays off. There is computer software geared to young children that is interactive and has educational value. Children can listen to good children's literature and then play games based on the book, which reinforces comprehension and literacy readiness. Engaging and educational math and science exploration software programs are available. Children can even begin writing and illustrating their own books. Videos and DVDs with interactive songs, creative movement, and musical games can be used to get children up and moving with the teacher and other children. Be very selective about what you show to the class. Always be aware that just because children like the video or DVD they bring to the classroom doesn't mean it is appropriate for a classroom setting. Be cautious about electronic worksheets and media offerings that do not represent what you want the children to experience. Make use of the many websites that help educators choose resources about teaching and caring for young children. Do your homework and preview everything first. Then use viewing time sparingly. Create some rules for yourself, such as presenting to children only media that you have previously screened for content and appropriateness. Make sure that all children have equal opportunities to explore and interact with the media. Be culturally sensitive. As children grow older, they will need to know how to use technology. In preschool, technology, like everything else, should be used with discretion and thoughtful moderation. Ask yourself if this information could be presented better in a concrete way without the technology. If the answer is yes, opt for an approach that benefits children the most (NAEYC and FRC 2012).

PRESCHOOL ACTIVITIES

Promote Emotional Development

❯ Be responsive to preschoolers' requests. Give lots of individual attention to all the children. Let children feel their self-worth. Create moments when you convey delight in each child.

❯ Make physical contact often. Touch helps all young children feel loved and nurtured and allows them to develop physically and cognitively.

❯ Keep noise levels low by providing small groups and quiet voices. A loud atmosphere is upsetting to some children and excites others.

❯ Allow preschoolers to have a comfort blanket, doll, or favorite object. They have learned to find comfort in the object when upset or ready to sleep.

❯ Hold young children and pat them on the back when they are upset to help calm them. Make physical contact and give hugs and pats on the back to show joy and approval.

❯ Massage backs and limbs as you talk to children in a soothing voice. Massage helps children relax and encourages them to go to sleep at naptime.

❯ Use words that let children know you care about and are interested in their thoughts and feelings.

❯ Empathize with children as they express their emotions.

FOSTERING RESILIENT PRESCHOOLERS

You can reinforce skills that help children cope when faced with adversity in life. The attributes that give children resilience—the ability to cope—stem from environments that teach children they are competent. A secure attachment with caregivers is an important protective factor in fostering resiliency. Many children and adults who persevere even in negative situations possess certain traits that allow them to thrive: they have an independence that allows them to forge ahead in difficult times, they have good control of their emotions and feel good about themselves, and they often have an interest or hobby that is a source of pride.

Parents and caregivers should help very young children learn how to manage difficult situations. Resilience can be taught by helping children build confidence in their ability to solve problems. Validating children's ideas and then testing their hypotheses lets them see they are resourceful. These activities help children apply critical-thinking skills. Encourage children to collect rocks, leaves, and seashells. Display the collection for others to see. Don't be surprised if the interest only lasts a few days. Group contributions, where several children collect items, add a social dimension that also contributes to resilience. Children who work as a team on a project—where they plan, execute with an adult's help, and review the outcome—realize their own unique capabilities. Children build confidence when they have meaningful involvement in an activity and see their contribution achieve the project's completion.

The bond between a child and one or more adults in the environment not only helps the child feel secure, safe, and loved but also gives the child an inner strength to combat adversity. A meaningful, caring relationship that the child can depend on, no matter the circumstance, provides support for healthy development. Families and caregivers are the model for personal identification. Children work harder for people they love and trust. Children who are emotionally secure and thrive socially gain the skills that will help them be more resilient in life.

PRESCHOOL ACTIVITIES

Support Resilience

❯ Invite small groups of children to build and paint a robot or alien (or anything they are interested in) from boxes and junk.

❯ Ask a group of older children to plan, build, and run a small carnival for younger children. Have only a few booths that the children can participate in creating and operating. A beanbag throw, a fishing game with magnetic fish, and a help-yourself snack are sufficient. Let children advertise, set it up, and clean up to conclude the sequence.

❯ Create an experience chart about a project after completion, emphasizing each child's work and contribution.

❯ Dig, plant, and care for a vegetable or flower garden as a class.

❯ Set up a restaurant in the dramatic play area. Let children create the menus, prepare and serve imaginary food, and collect payment from the guests.

❯ Create a grocery store using empty food boxes and cans (make sure the empty cans have smooth edges where the lid was removed). One or two children act as the cashiers, one puts the groceries in bags, and the rest are shoppers.

❯ Ask children what can be done to solve a problem after it has been identified. Encourage children to use their own resources to manage the situation, even if you, as an adult, recognize that their proposed solution may not work.

❯ Encourage children to seek help from their classmates or an adult when needed. Then you can offer suggestions while complimenting the children for trying to solve the problem on their own first.

CLOSING THOUGHTS

Emotional competence is a necessary component for being successful. Like everything in a child's life, emotional intelligence can be learned. The adults in a child's environment provide the nurturing that each child needs. Caregivers can help children cope in stressful situations and create the strength to be resilient. Good mental health is the result.

It is difficult to separate emotional abilities from social behavior. These two skills are intertwined. Children who are capable of managing their emotions are more likely to have the social skills necessary to work, play, and interact with others. Together, emotional and social competence create the most important foundation necessary for learning and succeeding in later school tasks (Singer 2007). The next chapter delves into how to help young children learn the social skills they will need to be successful in life.

CHAPTER 4

Social Development

Children need to learn how to get along with other people in a socially acceptable way during the early years. This need begins in infancy and continues throughout the preschool years. Young children are egocentric, which often means they want to do things their own way and want to possess the objects that surround them. The skills involved with delaying gratification, managing anger, and sharing with others do not come naturally. What does come naturally is a drive to be with others. Humans derive pleasure from interaction with people. Children learn to trust those who care for them by having their basic needs met. Once they feel safe and attached to their caregivers, they reach out to others for companionship. Children need to learn these skills to achieve success. Too often they receive little instruction on how to interact with others in a socially acceptable manner once they enter elementary school. The early years are critical, and your role in supporting children's social development is paramount.

Social skills are intertwined with emotional intelligence. It is hard to separate them, as a child's emotional state greatly influences how she relates to others. Children need to be able to manage their emotions and exhibit control when mingling and sharing space with others. This is not an easy task, but there are lots of ways you can encourage these skills. Socialization techniques should not be taught as independent skills. Instead, find the teachable moments and set up experiences that mirror real events to demonstrate skills that children need to gain social competence. This chapter is full of just such ideas.

SOCIAL DEVELOPMENT: THE INFANT AND TODDLER YEARS

As mentioned earlier, mirror neurons play a role in infants' learning to respond and socialize with others. They look at faces and mimic what they see. When an adult smiles, the infant smiles. At first, it is just a response. Adults—and older children—reward this behavior as they exclaim and smile again. The infant smiles back. Eventually, it becomes purposeful. Smiles pay a large role in human interaction. Infants learn to focus on faces and read expressions.

A majority of infant caregiving is about meeting the needs of the infant: they need to be fed when they are hungry, need to be kept warm and dry, and need to be nurtured to create feelings of security. Caregivers should be responsive to infant crying, which is their form of communication. Infants feel confident that their needs will be met when adults respond to their cries in a pleasant, soothing voice. Often it is hard to separate emotional needs and socialization for infants and toddlers. They are closely related, and one often affects the other (Lally 1998).

Children go through typical stages when learning how to socialize and play with others. Infants and young toddlers do not socialize on their own. They explore their immediate environment and move from one activity to another alone. They may be in close proximity to others, but there is no real interaction or awareness of other children. This stage is called *solitary play*. The next stage children go through is *parallel play*. There is no exact time when all children move into this stage. Children have their own timetable. In parallel play, children sit next to each other, often doing the same thing or playing with the same type of toy. Each may copy what the other child is doing, but basically they are still playing alone. Most older toddlers are in this stage. The next stages are *associative play* and *cooperative play*, which are defined in the preschool section of this chapter.

INFANT ACTIVITIES

Promote Social Development

❯ React to cries quickly with patience and understanding.

❯ Use diapering and feeding times to talk to infants face-to-face.

❯ Always hold an infant when giving him a bottle, even after he is able to sit independently.

❯ Use touch to help form bonds. Infant massage is soothing and helps solidify bonding with an adult.

❯ Hold and talk to infants often. Hold infants on your lap to read books, adjust clothing, or just to talk to them. Lightly bounce them on your knee as you pretend to give a horsey ride or recite a nursery rhyme.

- To make them feel secure, hold infants snugly against your body as you carry them.

- Teach socialization by playing with infants, using rhymes, fingerplays, and songs. Play games like "Peekaboo," "This Little Piggy," and "Patty-Cake" with a large smile close to the child's face as you gently move different body parts.

- Allow infants to explore your face, naming the parts that are being touched. In turn, touch and name their body parts. This interaction and touch helps infants socialize with you.

- Help infants make contact with other children. Keep groups of infants small for quiet, enjoyable interaction. Infants and toddlers are fascinated by other young children. Help them "talk" and be near to others.

- Keep contact with other adults casual and stress-free. Stay with the infant during a first-time meeting with an unknown adult. Help the child develop trust in the relationship before you leave.

- Give infants the same respectful alerts of upcoming transitions as you would older children: "I hear you starting to fuss; you must be getting hungry. I'm going to warm your bottle; then you can eat."

TODDLER ACTIVITIES

Promote Social Development

- Hold toddlers and explain their surroundings; patience is an important component in dealing with emerging personalities.

- Give toddlers lots of one-on-one time. They still need to be held and cuddled. Hold toddlers on your lap as you read books, recite nursery rhymes, or sing songs. Hug toddlers and talk to them often during the day.

- Help toddlers play with one other child, making sure there is sufficient equipment to allow each child to have the same toy if desired.

- Encourage interaction between toddlers as they learn swapping and sharing skills. Thank toddlers for giving toys to others, but do not expect them to always share.

- Create surroundings so toddlers can make choices and feel the power of being in control. The choices are theirs: "Do you want to play ball or build with blocks?"

- Avoid power struggles with toddlers. All toddlers say "No!" sometimes even when they mean "Yes."

- Help toddlers feel independent. Allow them to do small tasks for themselves and others. They can bring you their shoes to put on or carry the mail in from the mailbox.

- Model social skills you want toddlers to learn. Toddlers mimic what they see.

- Tell toddlers when they cooperate with you: "Wow! You picked up the doll and put her in the bed." "Thank you for holding Craig's hand."

- Rub children's backs at naptime. Close human contact is important.

TRANSITIONS WITH TODDLERS

Transitions are techniques that move children from one area or activity to another. They allow the adult to control the movement of individual children and groups. Transitions also let children know to stop an activity in one area and begin in another. Once toddlers are mobile, they should be asked to participate in transitions on their own accord, as opposed to you picking them up.

Toddlers need a warning about stopping play rather than an abrupt insistence to stop immediately: "We are leaving the park after two more times down the slide." "You have to put away the train soon to brush your teeth and take a nap." The following are suggestions that can help ease transitions and teach social skills.

TODDLER ACTIVITIES

Promote Socialization during Transitions

❯ Help a child take another child's hand to walk.

❯ Roll a ball to a child and congratulate him on catching it. Then ask him to carry it to the next place.

❯ Sing a song that gives directions to stand up, sit down, or walk or jump while moving to the next activity. Make up an easy tune that both you and the children can remember.

❯ Ask toddlers to walk, tiptoe, crawl, or run to you. Hugs let toddlers know they cooperated.

❯ Invite toddlers to pretend to be animals or cars as they move from one area to another.

GUIDANCE FOR TODDLERS

When toddlers interact with one another, there's bound to be conflict—it's to be expected from a group of children learning social skills! It's important to have an environment that allows for choice and provides multiples of favorite toys. Multiple toys that are alike promote peaceful parallel play. When toddlers experience a conflict over a toy, acknowledge the situation, and if a duplicate toy isn't available, do your best to redirect the children to different activities.

Some toddlers bite to try to get what they want. They do not have the words to say what they want, become frustrated, and bite. Monitoring toddlers and intervening before frustration sets in usually can prevent biting. When a toddler bites, comfort the child who was bitten and talk to the child who bit. Use vocabulary that explains what she wants, and then give her an object such as a dry sponge or an apple to bite: "Jessie, please don't bite. Biting hurts. If you need to bite, here is something you can bite."

Redirecting to another toy is helpful: "Tammy, biting hurts. Look at Tanner's face. Can you see he is upset? I know you wanted the red ball. Look, here is a colorful green ball. Can you roll it to me?" Toddlers are easily distracted, and taking them away from the area is beneficial.

Model language and encourage toddlers who bite to use simple words instead of biting. Their language skills are weak, but their feelings and desires are strong. Modeling the language they could be using and appealing to their empathy for the child who was bitten will help them move through this stage. Have them notice the crying child and, if possible, help them comfort that child. Then help talk them through the experience.

Teach toddlers to seek out a trusted adult to help them "get what they want when they want it." Once again, task-centered talking is a valuable tool: "Manny, you wanted the train. Do not bite Jeremy who is playing with the train. Biting hurts. Come tell me that you want the train. You could say, 'train,' and I will find another one for you to play with. See, here is a different train." For toddlers with more language, give them the exact words to use: "Tell Jeremy, 'I want to play with the train. Roll it to me, please.' If he says no, come get me. I will find you a different train to play with." This assistance has to be repeated frequently until the toddler can repeat and then initiate the statement.

Some adults think that if the child knew how much biting hurts, she would not bite. So, when a young child bites, the adult bites the child. This method should never be used with children. Young children are not yet able to understand that the pain they feel when bitten is related to the pain someone else feels when they bite. Rather, biting a child teaches her that biting is acceptable.

GROUP TIME WITH TODDLERS

Remember, group time should meet the maturation level of the individual child. Not all toddlers are ready for group experiences. Allow children to come in and out based on their interest and their attention span. Do not expect toddlers to sit quietly waiting for you or their classmates; keep group time very short and fun!

Promote Socialization during Group Time

❯ Comment on how children are sitting next to each other.

❯ Encourage children to hold hands as they walk from place to place, and comment when they do: "Jack and Kayla are holding hands as they walk to the door."

❯ Use songs and fingerplays that help toddlers touch each others' hands, fingers, and feet together while you give a running commentary: "We are touching pointer fingers."

❯ Encourage toddlers to look at each other as everyone does the same thing: "Everyone is wiggling their toes." "Look, all the children have their tongues out!"

❯ Comment when toddlers are socializing: "Gretchen is sitting next to Zoe." "Teddy and Craig are both playing with the train."

❯ Pass a toy around the circle. Help children give the toy to the next person. Chant as the toy moves: "Here comes the bear. Zoe is passing the bear. Tyler is passing the bear."

❯ Allow toddlers to help pass out napkins or cups to each child for snacks or meals. Show toddlers how to help other children when they are carrying something that is heavy or have too many objects to carry. Have two toddlers carry the wastebasket to collect trash: "You help Harry and hold this side of the wastebasket. Now you both are carrying the wastebasket together."

❯ Sing simple versions of "London Bridge Is Falling Down" and "Ring around the Rosie" so toddlers can practice touching each other.

SOCIAL DEVELOPMENT: THE PRESCHOOL YEARS

Some three-year-old children, especially girls, act more like older children. Others are still very babyish. Children should be with their peers for socialization, no matter how bright or mature they are. It does them a disservice to put them with older or younger children to meet their knowledge level. The very mature child can become a leader and the immature child can look to his maturer companions as role models. You can adjust activities and enriching experiences to the child's developmental level. Adult expectations must meet the child's current intellectual progress so the child can feel secure and confident.

Some preschoolers are still in the parallel play stage. They tend to play next to others but do not truly socialize. With maturation and experience, they will move to the next stage of *associative play*. In associative play, children are beginning to interact with one another. They can play side by side and use the same toys. Their play is often haphazard and jumps from one topic to another as they converse. They can share the blocks and build next to each other, but each is creating her own imaginary structure. In the dramatic play area, each child may be taking care of a doll and feeding the doll, sharing the sinks and tables, and interacting both verbally and with similar scenarios; but the children aren't really playing together. Each has his own imaginative story line. Often during associative play a leader emerges who tells others what to do to create a loosely organized play experience.

The next play stage is *cooperative play*. Many older preschoolers move into cooperative play. In this stage, the children truly cooperate with each other to create a building together or pretend to be a family. The play is organized and all are interacting toward one goal together. Children have assigned roles and exchange ideas as the scenario morphs. The children are socializing, communicating, and working in tandem.

Children go through these stages on their own timetable. Some childrens' personalities prevent them from reaching cooperative play while in preschool. Also, children may exhibit parallel play in a situation where they are unfamiliar with the other children and cooperative play at home with siblings. No matter what stage they are in, children benefit from the play activities that are embedded daily into the curriculum.

Focus on teaching social skills as part of every activity during the day. To be of value, social skills need to be learned not in isolation, but as an integral part of everything that is happening. Socialization is an integral part of how children relate to adults and to each other. What better place to relax and learn how to interact with others?

Children who don't learn how to get along with others in the first few years may have problems their entire lives. Often there is a snowball effect. The child is disliked and excluded from play for not having the skills to get along with other people. When the child is excluded, she doesn't have the opportunities to practice social skills, and often the undesirable behavior escalates as a means to get

attention. Adults have a responsibility to intervene to help the child learn socially acceptable ways to interact with others in the early years. Young children who engage in activities that promote social skills and learn how to solve problems in getting along with others will likely go on to be productive, social adults. You need to look for the teachable moments and create activities that promote social skills.

In the United States, individuality and independence are held in high regard, often at the expense of cooperation. Yet good social skills—including cooperation—are critical to success in life. It's important to keep in mind what your values are and what children need to succeed when encouraging self-help skills and social skills. For example, in Japan, teamwork is valued more than independence, and cooperation is taught from an early age. Young children learn how to work in small groups. Children are expected to learn how to get along with others cooperatively. Team building is a way of life. Conversely, teachers in the United States often tell children to keep their hands to themselves and to find their own space (an area around each person that belongs to them alone), and they encourage a measure of competition in children. These tendencies often lead to a lack of consideration for other people. You can help children find a balance between the two with a mindful emphasis on being a member of the group. Some children (and adults) do not know how to make friends. Children may hit or grab a toy to get the other child's attention. That child needs to learn how to approach others and ask to play. It's important to teach social skills in many different ways to children and to provide opportunities for children to experience cooperation with others. There are countless opportunities to support social skills during a typical preschooler's day. As illustrated in the suggestions that follow, cleanup time provides a golden opportunity to promote working as a team.

PRESCHOOL ACTIVITIES

Promote Cooperation

> Have two children sweep the floor: one pushes the broom while the other holds the dustpan.

> Encourage two children to work together on puzzles, manipulative toys, or at the computer.

> Set up two children to paint together at the easel using the same paper. Murals allow more children to interact together to create one product.

> Suggest that children carry wastebaskets, watering cans, or heavy pails of supplies together.

> Bounce or roll balls back and forth between two children. Roll balls to others in a circle, calling the name of the recipient. Throw beanbags or paper wads to vary the activity.

> Assign one child to pick up the dolls and a second to wrap them in blankets and put them in the bed.

> Set up an assembly line to put away blocks. Line up the children and have one pick up the block and pass it down the line to the last child, who puts it into the block storage cabinet.

> Let several children collaborate to pick up colored blocks: "Anthony, please pick up the yellow cubes. Anna, you pick up the blue cubes, please."

TRANSITIONS WITH PRESCHOOLERS

Preschool children need to know when one activity or portion of the day has ended and another is ready to begin. Transitions help them stop the play they are engaged in and provide a bridge to the next task. Just as with toddlers, preschoolers need to have a warning. When a child is focused on an activity, such as block building or painting, it is difficult to stop immediately. This is especially true when playing outdoors. By giving the child a warning that the play is about to end, the child has time to move the scenario to a conclusion or finish a physical interaction. This avoids a lot of upset and defiant behavior. Transitions are fun, and by using a variety of techniques, you can easily engage the children's cooperation.

Promote Social Skills during Transitions

➤ Encourage cooperation by using songs, balls, and verbal games to move children from one activity to the next.

➤ Have a puppet whisper to each child where to go when it is time to move: "Shhhh! Tiptoe quietly to the door."

➤ Toss or roll a ball to a child who is paying attention. Then give the direction of where to go.

➤ Give directions using color, identifying clothing, names of the children, rhyming words, or first letters in their name to indicate who is to move: "If you are wearing green, you may get your coat on to go outside."

➤ Create twenty-second plays that two children can act out together before moving to the next area. Nursery rhymes lend themselves to this very well. One child can be the woman and one the dog as you recite "Old Mother Hubbard," and then the two can go wash their hands.

➤ Use songs, nursery rhymes, and fingerplays to help children cooperate. Use riddles and chants like Ella Jenkins's "Stop and Go" or a song like "Tiptoe through the Tulips."

➤ Be a mime. Create pretend images. Illustrate what you are talking about with gestures.

  • "Carry this ball carefully to the sink to wash your hands." As you say this, pretend to hand the child a large round ball.

  • "Tiptoe on these rocks in the stream as you go to the door." Demonstrate stepping carefully from rock to rock.

  • "Hold this baby kitten carefully as you walk to the rug and sit down." Cup your hands and gently place the pretend kitten into the child's hands.

  • "Here is an egg. See if you can carry it without breaking and go lie down on your mat." Gently place a pretend egg into the child's cupped hands.

COOPERATIVE LANGUAGE IN PRESCHOOL

Use words that incorporate the vocabulary you want the children to demonstrate with behavior. They will learn to understand the concepts from hearing you describe expected actions.

• "You heard me ask everyone to walk to the door. Lindsay listened and is cooperating."

• "These two boys are cooperating together and are building a skyscraper."

• "Andy and Phil cooperated to clean up the play area together."

• "With teamwork, these blocks were picked up quickly."

• "Everyone was a good listener and used inside voices."

• "Leslie cooperated and helped everyone clean up the pretend area together."

BUILDING SOCIAL SKILLS IN PRESCHOOL

Children need to be touched and hugged often by the important adults in their lives. Hug and cuddle children to teach them to hug and reach out to other children and adults. Such human contact is essential to developing good self-esteem, which can translate into good social skills. Children need to feel wanted and loved. They enjoy hugging, giggling, and holding hands with others. Just as children learn about inappropriate touches, adults must teach them that it is sometimes all right to be touched by others. This will prevent anger when one child brushes against the next or sits too close. Plan activities, such as opening a surprise bag or feeling for objects inside a box, where children sit together in cramped areas. Explain how touching in such situations is acceptable. Crowd together in a corner to read a book. Play games and sing songs that help children touch each other in socially acceptable ways. When children interact with others in an acceptable fashion, comment on these behaviors so they will repeat them in the future. Keep comments specific.

- "You cooperated with Julie to build a house together in the block area."

- "Sharing the car with Russell made the game more fun."

- "You helped Joey carry the box."

- "Everyone held hands as we sang 'Ring around the Rosie.'"

- "Damico buttoned Jerome's sweater. Thank you, Damico!"

Getting along with others requires children to understand the feelings and moods of others as well as learn how to share and use materials. Spend time teaching children to look at faces for clues. Model empathy and express your feelings appropriately. Respect children's feelings. If a child doesn't want to participate in the group activity, ask why, but don't force the child to participate. Pro-

vide other group activities that this child will enjoy. It's important that each child know and practice the skills necessary to get along with other children.

PRESCHOOL ACTIVITIES

Promote Social Development

❯ Use songs that promote clapping, holding hands, swinging arms, and jumping in pairs. Change actions in popular songs, such as "If You're Happy and You Know It" and "Put Your Finger in the Air," to allow children to touch each other appropriately.

❯ Change the words of fingerplays to practice touching others. Chant "Open, Shut Them" and clap hands with a neighbor rather than themselves. Let one child touch the fingers of a partner as you recite, "Where Is Thumbkin?"

❯ Teach children how to touch others appropriately with games like "London Bridge Is Falling Down," "Ring around the Rosie," "Skip to My Lou," and "The Farmer in the Dell." Teach creative movement activities and dances so children learn to value others' space. Help children tolerate "good touches" from others.

❯ Read books that show animals and people interacting amicably. Read stories, such as *Three Little Pigs* and *Chicken Little*. Discuss the process the characters of the story used to work together.

❯ Promote good touching skills using fingerplays and nursery rhymes. Help children act out "Jack and Jill," "Hey, Diddle Diddle," or "Little Miss Muffet."

❯ Play multiple forms of tag where children lightly touch others on the shoulder or arm to tag or choose the next person.

❯ Use games and activities that identify body language and facial expressions. Talk about when Alex looks angry as not the time to ask him to share the toy train.

- Put on a little play with another adult or puppets. Show children squabbling over a toy or pushing a child out of line. Stop the action and ask children for their solutions. Act out each of their proposed solutions. Discuss with the group the pros and cons of each.

- Provide cooperative activities in which children share a job and depend on each other for completion. Carry a heavy jug of water to pour into the water table or paint a picture together. One child washes the table while the other dries.

- Work on hard puzzles or large floor puzzles together. Design a large block structure as a group to practice getting along with others.

- Greet new children or guests with a handshake song. Ask several children to show them around the classroom or playground.

PRACTICING SOCIAL SKILLS IN PRESCHOOL LEARNING CENTERS

Socialization is a natural outgrowth of play in classroom interest centers. When children argue and learn to cooperate as they play, they are rehearsing the skills they will need for getting along with others in the outside world. The difference is that creative play is comfortable, somewhat predictable, and children have the help of adults to manage the situation.

Children have opportunities to interact with other children and practice social skills while engaged in play. Through play, children explore not only ideas but also personality traits such as self-control, persistence, and paying attention. They can even learn how to argue and control anger. Sometimes children model their play on the behavior of the adults in their lives or what they have seen on television and in movies. After watching superheroes save the day, they want to be in control of the play. They have to learn how to negotiate with others if they want to be the person in power. Teach them to use communication skills and to compromise.

Children recreate their lives in the family-living or dramatic-play area and try out family dynamics there as well. They learn to be nurturers when they take care of dolls or cook for other children. They practice taking on social roles—customer, clerk, server, and so on—that will be important for their future independence. The block area offers many opportunities for children to work cooperatively and share materials to create structures and landscapes. A library area with large pillows or beanbag chairs that encourage children to sit together to read a book provides yet another social interaction. Water and sand tables are perfect places to work in close proximity to others and use and share the same pouring and measuring implements. Easels, manipulatives, and cognitive toys can be arranged so that several children are interacting. Even computers can be used for social skill building activities by adding two or three chairs so several children can participate and discuss the software. The following list highlights aspects of social skills children learn as they play together in interest areas:

- Communication skills
- Leadership skills
- Team building skills
- Working together toward a common goal
- Sharing materials and supplies
- Sitting and working next to other children

Children need guidance as they attempt to socialize. You are there as their support and coach. Observe each child to assess his level of skills, and step in to assist when the child needs help. When children exhibit social competence, validate their social skills. Be sincere when pointing out good group dynamics. Try to point out different social situations to confirm positive behavior, as children pick up insincerity when they are always praised for the same behavior.

Here are some examples of ways to validate social skills:

- "You and Alisa are cooperating on building this village."

- "The three of you have worked well together."

- "Jerry, what a nice job you did helping Suzi build the wall."

- "Hannah and Justin shared the task and helped each other feed the mice."

- "You cooperated by taking turns with the magnet."

- "You helped Ramon put on his tie."

- "Thank you for giving Natalie a turn with the high-heeled shoes!"

- "What a nice gesture to let Sarah sit at the restaurant table."

- "I like the way you girls are sharing the glue."

- "I am so glad to see you gave Gracie the yellow marker when you were finished with it."

- "You worked together and found a way to keep paint off the wall."

SNACK AND MEALS IN PRESCHOOL

Snack and mealtime should be a relaxed period of socialization and conversation. Each child's individual preferences should be honored. As they're able and as the situation allows, invite children to help prepare to eat. This participation contributes to their feeling of being a part of the group. While you eat with the children, create conversations by asking open-ended questions and encouraging the children to ask questions of each other. In group care, children eat together and conversation should be rich and interactive—this is an important part of the child's day. The adult is the model and helps engage children in conversation in a relaxed atmosphere. This one activity encompasses not just socialization; it also helps children feel independent, helps them feel good about their abilities, and can have an academic component if the conversation lends to that. Preparing to eat can also involve one-to-one correspondence when children are asked to set the table, putting one napkin at each seat. Once again, all aspects of child development converge.

Encourage Skill Development at Snacktime

❱ Teach children how to use utensils and how to pass bowls of food from one child to another.

❱ Supply small pitchers for children to pour their own drink, and then pass the pitcher to the next child.

❱ Let children count out their own portion of pretzels, carrot sticks, or apple slices from a container in the middle of the table.

❱ Let each child share their likes and dislikes as well as their experiences with food in other situations. The adults keep the conversation going by asking questions about where the food came from or providing facts that will stimulate replies from the children: "Have you ever heard of a raisin tree? I don't think there is such a tree. How are raisins made?" "Did you know that pretzels come in many shapes? What shapes of pretzels have you eaten?"

❱ Use facts about the snack to form a riddle for the children to work on together to reveal what food will be served.

SOCIAL DEVELOPMENT AND GUIDANCE IN PRESCHOOL

Some common scenes in preschool group care settings are ripe for social learning. The following section addresses these and provides support for the adult working with preschool children.

When a child pulls a toy away from another child, caregivers often take away the toy. This only teaches that the biggest and most powerful (the adult) wins. It sets the child up to continue the misbehavior of grabbing toys. Instead, use problem-solving techniques to help guide the child. Use discussion along with consequences—such as a brief period to regroup—after a child hits another child to get a desired toy. Accompany this with helping the child learn how to deal with a situation of wanting a toy another child possesses.

Frequently, adults say, "Use your words" when children are in disagreement and are not verbalizing the problem or their intentions or desires. In the beginning, this direction is too vague (see chapters 6 and 7 for more information about language development). Young children need the exact words to use. This assistance has to be repeated frequently until the words come easily. Even then, the child will often still need a reminder: "What should you say to get the toy you want to play with?" Help children generate solutions if they are still unable to verbalize their thoughts. Here are some examples:

- "You could ask to play with the toy."

- "You could find another toy just like the one Bobby has."

- "You could take turns. Ask Danny, 'When may I have a turn?'"

- "You could find a way to play with the toy together."

- And always included, "You could ask me, your teacher, to help you."

Adults tend to separate children who have quarreled. If we really are serious about teaching prosocial skills, then we should look for ways to help these same children work cooperatively. Assess the anger levels when one child hurts another. Once they're calmed down, have the children play or work together: "You need to help Jason rebuild his sand mountain." "Both of you are in charge of putting away the sand toys. Let's see if you can each pick up ten toys!" "Here is a puzzle that nobody has put together. Let's see how fast you two can complete the puzzle and put it on the shelf."

Preschool classrooms sometimes include children who are continuously aggressive even after coaching and support. Whatever is the cause of aggression in a child, caregivers must assess how the behavior affects others in the room. If other children in the class are afraid of the aggressive child, their vigilance causes stress and prevents them from fully participating in the day's activities.

The aggressive child, meanwhile, is also experiencing stress. The brain's wiring may go awry, and a lack of impulse control and violence can become the norm. Ineffective interventions that fail to stop the aggressive behavior often result in the child being socially ostracized, which can then lead to bullying. However, with early intervention using effective age-appropriate guidance, conflict resolution, and discipline techniques, this cycle can be stopped. All children need your support. Don't hesitate to seek outside expert help.

Teach children to stand up for themselves. We want children to develop the courage to assert their rights. Help children who are being picked on learn the words to use with an aggressive child. Learning to tell another child "Stop hitting me!" or "No, I don't want to do that!" may help the child to take control of the situation. Modeling the language the child needs to use in adverse situations is important. Such intervention will have to be repeated often until the child discovers the ability to use the words independently. The child also needs to know that she can come to you for assistance. This is not tattling but teaching coping skills. Imagine how important this will be when children are pressured to use drugs as teens!

APOLOGIES AND PRESCHOOLERS

Adults often make children say, "I'm sorry," every time they have a negative interaction with another child. The truth of the matter is they are not sorry, and the phrase soon becomes meaningless. Children hit, say they are sorry, and go about their play, not taking responsibility for their actions. Often the act is repeated in a short span of time. One useful strategy requires both empathy and problem solving techniques. After commenting on the feelings of the injured child and assisting with words that could be used instead of physical aggression, ask the child to work at not repeating the behavior. Provide the child with an alternative action or a different activity. Don't expect the offending behaviors to immediately disappear. This teachable moment will occur again. It's important to repeat this assistance until the process becomes a permanent part of behavior.

PROMOTING SOCIALIZATION FOR PRESCHOOLERS DURING GROUP TIME

Small group or circle time is a wonderful time of day to promote social skills. Since young children do not learn by being lectured to, provide activities that teach them to touch and share, and put socialization lessons into understandable context. Use the following ideas to try new things, and allow your creativity to take you in new directions.

PRESCHOOL ACTIVITIES

Promote Socialization during Group Time

➤ Put two children together as partners. Give each pair one set of rhythm sticks, ribbons, or streamers. Play music and show them how to use the equipment together.

➤ Have one windmill, one tambourine, or one paper plate for every two children. Have them move the object together with music or let them work together to create ways of manipulating the article: "Can one of you hold the windmill and the other make it go around and around?" "See if you can both hold the tambourine and shake it." "Can you find three ways to make the paper plate twirl around?"

➤ Stand in a circle. Let a child create a unique handshake, and have everyone in the circle repeat it with the next person in the circle. Give each child a turn at being the leader.

➤ Place a piece of newspaper between two children. Have them walk around it stepping on each corner. Have them change directions. Give them multiple directions to each place a body part on the newspaper. Let them hold hands and jump over the newspaper. Continue with directions that call for them to work cooperatively.

❯ Increase self-esteem and help children feel accepted by hearing compliments. Have children stand in a circle and say nice comments about the child next to them. Teach children to respond with "Thank you!"

❯ Give one bottle of bubbles and a wand to two children. Encourage them to blow bubbles. Ask each child to count the bubbles the other child blows.

❯ Have the birthday child sit in a chair as the class shares the child's positive attributes. Write them on a paper for the child to keep.

❯ Have pairs of children figure out ways to transport a Hula-Hoop, Frisbee, or large box together from one side of the room to another. They may choose to roll it on its rim, slide it across the floor, or carry it as they hop, jump, skip, or crawl from one side to another. The only rule is the object can't be thrown. You'll be delighted at their creativity!

❯ Have all children stand in a line across the room and not move their feet. Ask the children to transport a paper plate from one end of the room to the other by handing it to the next child in line.

❯ Have pairs of children stand back-to-back (touching) and walk across the room as a unit.

❯ Have the children sit in a circle, take turns rolling a ball to another child, saying something nice or expressing feelings related to social skills: "It hurts my feelings when Barb won't sit next to me." "I don't like when Joe pushes me." "I like when Sally plays ball with me."

❯ With the children sitting in a circle, pass beanbags or pennies while chanting or singing, "Pass the Penny," "Who Stole the Cookie from the Cookie Jar?" or "Button, Button, Who's Got the Button?"

❯ Take a broken umbrella and remove the material to use as a small parachute. Have four to six children hold part of the circular material. Have them move together in a circle then turn and walk the other way. Put a ball on the parachute and have children work together to roll the ball to each person without letting it hit the floor.

CLOSING THOUGHTS

Children are born not knowing how to interact with others in a socially acceptable manner. They have to learn through experience. The early years are the time children learn the skills to get along with others and cooperate with the adults in their lives. Skills come gradually and need to be reinforced and practiced over time. Possessing social skills is a key to later educational success and success in life.

The curriculum of the early years must include teaching children to cooperate, to follow directions, to keep their hands to themselves, to get along with other children, and to resolve conflicts. For children to thrive and be ready to learn in an educational setting, they must have social competence. Once they have acquired this attribute, they are ready to use their bodies and minds to the fullest.

Physical Development

With typical growth and ability, a child's physical development usually follows predictable and sequential patterns. Motor skills develop from the head down and from the midline out to the extremities. Large muscles develop before small muscles—muscles in the legs and arms develop before those in the fingers and hands. Infants gain control in their necks first, and their fingers are the last body part to complete muscular development. They learn to hold their heads up before they learn how to crawl.

Physical development is determined by both genetic inheritance and environmental influences. The brain's window of opportunity for physical development is the first two years of life, with all areas wired by age five, but improvement and refinement continue until mastery through the teen years. A child can be born with the musculature to be a great athlete, but unless she has the opportunity to develop the muscles and skills for a sport, her athletic potential will never be realized. Continue the enhancement of motor skills through exercise and practice. It is harder to learn a new skill in later life, but it can be done with perseverance.

It takes a complicated coordination of brain circuitry to accomplish muscular tasks. Multiple neurons controlling various muscles have to synchronize with thoughts of what we are attempting to accomplish with the movement. Over time, we develop *muscle memory*, which means that we do not have to think about reaching our hand out, opening our fingers, lowering our arm to table level, grasping a pen, and closing our fingers in order to pick up a pen. We practiced grasping objects as infants, refined the technique as toddlers, used it over and over as preschoolers, and now it just comes naturally without having to think. You want a pen and you pick it up.

There are two major kinds of muscle development. Development of the large muscle groups, referred to as *gross-motor skills*, comes from walking or running with the legs or waving and throwing with the arms. *Fine-motor skills* refers to small muscle growth developed through smiling, grasping, and kicking. We need to combine fine-motor skills with hand-eye coordination to write or tie a bow.

PHYSICAL DEVELOPMENT: THE INFANT AND TODDLER YEARS

Infants have reflexive motor movement the minute they are born. Soon they learn to raise their heads to look around. Their reflexive grasp becomes purposeful as they try to reach for objects they see. They have a strong inner motivation to move. Most infants go through the same sequence of skills: rolling over before rocking on their knees, crawling before walking. Some infants walk at eight months and others not until eighteen months. All are within the normal range. When children first walk is determined by their genetic background, their health, and available space for moving. Consult developmental milestone charts to monitor physical development. If a child has motor delays of three months or more, parents should discuss this with their pediatrician.

Infants depend on adults to keep them fed,

clean, and dry. They need room to exercise and stimulate their young muscles in accordance with their natural flow of active time and sleep. Each infant has an individual schedule of needs for being fed, napped, or changed.

Sleep is necessary for brain maturation and growth. The brain processes information during sleep, and research now shows how critical this processing time is for strengthening memory and rehearsing information (Schiller 2010). Many families keep TV programs, music, or videos playing while children are sleeping. It is important to make certain the area where the child is sleeping is dark and quiet. According to the Kaiser Family Foundation, 19 percent of children under two have a TV in their room (Rideout, Hamel, and Kaiser Family Foundation 2006). Share this important

information with the families of children in your care and encourage them to keep their children's bedrooms quiet at bedtime.

Children today are less physically active from infancy on than their parents were at the same age (Doheny 2004). Infants spend time belted in infant seats, baby swings, and high chairs. Toddlers often sit in front of a television or computer, or are strapped into a car seat. Therefore, it is imperative that people who care for children incorporate multiple physical elements into the day.

INFANT ACTIVITIES

Meet Their Physical Needs

❯ Provide a clean padded space on the floor for wiggling, rolling, and scooting. This helps infants develop muscle groups. An infant should have thirty minutes of tummy time over the course of a day. Motivate movements with large colorful balls, baby gyms, and clean, safe toys. When infants are alert, mobiles, mirrors, and bright pictures should be in their proximity. Place an infant under a mobile or play gym for short periods of time. This challenges the child to reach for the objects he sees. Get down on the floor next to him and encourage him to interact with you as well as the nearby objects.

❯ Place cribs in a quiet area with dim light to allow sufficient rest required by growing bodies.

❯ Feed infants on demand. A rocking chair lends comfort when giving a bottle.

❯ Hold children who have moved to solid food while feeding for the first few months to give the one-on-one nurturing that is optimum. When they are able to sit up, short periods in a high chair provide a good place for feeding.

❯ Once they move to finger foods, help the child feed herself by placing small bites on the high-chair tray. As she becomes proficient, give her a spoon.

❯ Create places that are safe for infants to crawl around in or to pull themselves up to stand or attempt to walk. Padded or carpeted areas allow for many falls without harm.

❯ Place large colorful toys within arm's reach for cruisers and beginning walkers.

❯ Provide rattles and toys that are easy to hold to help infants learn to grasp.

❯ Shake a rattle or call the child's name as you stand on one side to encourage him to turn his head. Go to the other side and repeat the noise to exercise neck muscles.

❯ Give infants stacking toys and various sizes of pots and pans to explore once they can sit up. Show them how to bang lids and how to put one pan inside or on top of another.

❯ Place a light receiving blanket on top of the infant's head. Teach her to lift the blanket as you play "Peekaboo."

SUDDEN INFANT DEATH SYNDROME (SIDS)

Since many infants begin group care as young as six weeks of age, it is important to know how to keep them both healthy and safe. Young children are fully dependent on you, the adult. Sudden infant death syndrome (SIDS) can be prevented in most cases. The danger period for SIDS is primarily between two and four months. After six months the majority of infants have outgrown the danger zone for SIDS; however, parents and caregivers can't let down their guard (Mayo Foundation for Medical Education and Research 2011). The following recommendations come from the American SIDS Institute (2009):

• "Place infants to sleep on their backs, even though they may sleep more soundly on their stomachs. Infants who sleep on their stomachs and sides have a much higher rate of SIDS than infants who sleep on their backs."

- "Place infants to sleep in a baby bed with a firm mattress. There should be nothing in the bed but the baby—no covers, no pillows, no bumper pads, no positioning devices, and no toys. Soft mattresses and heavy coverings are associated with the risk for SIDS."

- "Do not place [a] baby to sleep in an adult bed. Typical adult beds are not safe for babies. Do not fall asleep with [a] baby on a couch or in a chair."

- "Do not overclothe the infant while she sleeps. Just use enough clothes to keep the baby warm without having to use covers. Keep the room at a temperature that is comfortable for you. Overheating an infant may increase the risk for SIDS."

- "Avoid exposing the infant to tobacco smoke. . . . The greater the exposure to tobacco smoke, the greater the risk of SIDS."

- "Avoid exposing the infant to people with respiratory infections."

Keep up on the research, and share information with families. For more information, visit the American SIDS Institute's website at www.sids.org.

INFANT HEAD POSITIONING

If infants spend too much time on their backs, they may develop a flat head. Infants' skulls are very soft, and the bones can be affected by pressure. Infants also have weak neck muscles and tend to turn their heads to one side and leave it in that position when placed on their backs. If infants always turn their heads to the same side, the skull may flatten. A little bit of flattening goes away on its own. More serious flattening may be permanent, but it will not affect an infant's brain or normal development. To prevent an infant from getting a flat head, change the position of the head each day while she sleeps and make sure the child does not lie in the crib for long periods of time when awake.

INFANT ACTIVITIES

Prevent Flat Heads

❯ Alternate the infant's orientation with the head or foot of the crib. Change with each new nap. Check to make sure that the child is always looking out into the room.

❯ On a wall in a play area, attach an unbreakable mirror or photographs of family members at an infant's eye level. Lay the nonmobile infant near the mirror or photos, orienting her head so the object is in her line of sight. Alternate the child's position each day so that she orients her head to the left on one day and to the right on the next.

❯ Stand to one side of the infant and call his name. Stand and talk to him as he turns his head toward your voice.

INFANT MOVEMENT AND EXERCISE

Most pediatricians feel that infants don't need formal exercise programs to help them develop the musculature and coordination needed to roll over, crawl, cruise, and walk. Yet exercise programs for infants are touted in the media and advertised to parents. Consult the child's pediatrician before embarking on an infant exercise program.

Avoid walkers, jumpers, exersaucers, and other paraphernalia that have young nonambulatory infants immobilized for long periods of time. Use swings only for short diversions of less than fifteen minutes. Swings restrict the natural movement of limbs. Walkers, jumpers, and bouncers not only restrict muscle development, but also put too much weight on hips, knees, and ankles.

Here are some ideas for exercising young joints and muscles. Have parents check with their pediatrician before trying any of these suggestions:

- Assist the infant in sitting. Grasp her hands as she holds your thumbs and gently help her into a sitting position. Repeat five times.

- Help him roll over gently as you support his head and back.

- When the infant is alert and on her back—while diapering, for example—gently pedal her legs as if on a bicycle.

- Help the infant gently wave his arms up and down and from side to side.

- Let the infant hold your thumbs and help her slowly extend her arms and then bring them back to her chest. Never force the movement (Polak 2009).

THE INDOOR ENVIRONMENT FOR INFANTS AND TODDLERS

Both equipment and the room arrangement should reflect infants' and toddlers' needs. The day's schedule revolves not only around children's physical requirements, but also around meeting children's cognitive, sensory, and motor needs. The atmosphere should be calm. The room should be light and airy and kept at a comfortable temperature. Pathways have to be kept clear of clutter. There should not be too much that is stimulating. Keep only one or two posters and photographs at eye level. Too much visual stimulation is overwhelming.

Toys need to be large and geared for the age group in the room. Make sure to rotate toys often to keep young children interested. Check that there are no small parts that could be a choking hazard. The room should be arranged so that children have easy access to floor time. Since each infant or toddler has his own timetable for sleeping, eating, and wakefulness, the cribs should be separated from the crawling, walking, and floor areas. Cleanliness is paramount, with toys and surfaces washed and sanitized daily.

Infants and toddlers have extremely short attention spans, so plan the day to keep them engaged. Don't think that just because they are young, lesson plans are not important. Make sure you have a time for music, for outdoor exposure, for movement, and to play with toys. Schedule sensory exploration and stories. Lap time with fingerplays and nursery rhymes should be interspersed throughout the day. Napping, diapering, and feeding are all part of the day's curriculum. And don't forget the most important ingredient—you. Your interaction with the infants and toddlers is imperative. Infants' brains are very active and need you to provide nurturing, communication, and care.

Support Physical Play Indoors

❯ Arrange a safe area to promote standing and walking skills. Walkways should be kept clear of clutter. Infants and toddlers have very short attention spans, so their interest in a toy will be fleeting. It is easy for the area to become cluttered and hazardous in a very short time.

❯ Place toys on shelves or in tubs that children can reach. Toys should be accessible to older infants and toddlers without requiring an adult to get the desired toy. Provide containers to dump out and refill. Young children love repetitive action.

❯ Provide an array of pull toys, push toys, transportation toys, large blocks, and balls.

❯ Add musical toys and instruments that require an action from a child to produce the noise.

❯ Provide toy brooms and mops. Toddlers mimic what they see. Let them help you dust, pull clothes out of baskets, and help with other chores. They will think it is fun.

❯ Create low obstacle routes for children to navigate. Cushions, tunnels, and cardboard boxes to crawl under, over, and through attract toddlers and stimulate physical movement. Pile firm pillows and encourage young children to crawl over "the mountain."

❯ Prevent climbing on chairs and tables by providing safe, low climbing apparatus.

❯ Periodically lead creative movement to music. Keep the activity short.

❯ Furnish low water and sand tables with containers that are easy to fill and pour.

❯ Provide low easels and large paper along with easy-to-manipulate brushes and no-spill containers at toddler height.

❯ Help toddlers tear paper into pieces and put them in a bucket. Have blunt scissors available as they mature.

❯ Have cloth and board books available for children to practice handling and turning pages.

❯ Provide nontoxic crayons and markers to use on big pieces of paper.

❯ Provide small boxes, and encourage children to pick them up, stack them, or carry them around.

❯ Teach older toddlers to pour their own drinks using small pitchers. Let them use craft sticks to spread butter or cream cheese on crackers. Provide a cupcake liner with dip, and teach them to dip pretzels and veggie sticks in the dip.

FINGERPLAYS FOR INFANTS AND TODDLERS

Fingerplays give children an opportunity to talk and move simultaneously. Fingerplays exercise arm, hand, and finger musculature. Children use multiple parts of their brains simultaneously when hand and body motions are added as adults recite fingerplays or sing songs.

In the beginning, adults have to manipulate the young child's fingers and move them to the words. Infants delight in listening to the rhythm as you recite the chant and move their hands and arms. Exaggerate the singsong quality of fingerplays to excite infants and toddlers. Fingerplays help the fingers, hands, and arms develop more control. They are developing the musculature to write. Here are favorites of very young children:

• "Where Is Thumbkin?"

• "This Little Piggy"

• "I'm a Little Teapot"

• "Open, Shut Them"

• "Itsy Bitsy Spider"

• "Little Bunny Foo Foo"

SPENDING TIME OUTDOORS WITH INFANTS AND TODDLERS

Taking infants and toddlers outside is an important part of their day. When weather permits, outdoor time allows very young children to learn in a different environment. Nature provides an endless array of learning opportunities. The outdoors presents smells, sounds, and sights that are ever changing and rich. Aside from the educational components, sunshine and open spaces appeal to the emotions and provide freedom for exploration. Comment on the feel of wind blowing and the heat of sun on their arms. Help infants and toddlers touch natural growing items like tree bark and leaves and smell flowers and leaves. It is a different experience when they see growing, living things.

INFANT & TODDLER ACTIVITIES

Support Physical Play Outdoors

❯ Make walks interactive by stopping and letting infants and toddlers touch and feel leaves, sticks, and tree bark. Bring a paper bag. Have the children bend down or reach up to get leaf specimens, sticks, and rocks to put into the bag.

❯ Place a large blanket on the grass, and let infants enjoy tummy time. Roll a ball to an infant who can sit up. Aim the ball at their feet some of the time and encourage them to kick.

❯ Pull an infant who can sit up in a wagon, and teach the infant to hold on to the sides.

❯ Visit parks and playgrounds that offer baby swings and low climbing equipment. Place infants on the slide and hold them as they slowly descend. Low slides are as much fun for toddlers to go up as to come down. Climbing and sliding are enjoyed over and over.

❯ As the child becomes ambulatory, provide riding toys that use her feet to make the toy move. Older toddlers can learn to pedal a tricycle.

❯ Provide low climbing equipment that young toddlers can crawl over and under.

❯ Use steps to provide a new dimension to exercising young muscles. Help children go up and down stairs, first crawling and then walking. They will be fascinated with this new venture, and it helps improve balance.

❯ Play music and invite toddlers to dance in a safe, grassy area.

❯ Play in sandboxes to encourage fingers and hands to develop dexterity as young toddlers put the sand in cups and pails. Teach that sand cannot go into their mouths or be thrown.

❯ Add water to soil or sand to change the play. Toddlers like to dig in mud. It is messy, but it helps develop large and small arm and hand muscles and hand-eye coordination.

❯ Add a variety of push toys, such as toy lawn mowers. Take pull toys outside.

❯ Let toddlers help water and dig in a garden. Pulling up carrots or picking beans is fun and easy for very young children. Watch for ants and ladybugs on plants. Point out leaves that have been eaten by insects. Butterfly plants, which are easy to grow, are breeding grounds for hungry caterpillars. Teach young children to watch but not touch.

PHYSICAL DEVELOPMENT: THE PRESCHOOL YEARS

Children need to move and be active in many ways to reach their full physical potential. Preschoolers are building on what they already know and are going from the simple to the complex. Parents and caregivers can support children by providing a variety of experiences that challenge different muscle groups and help each child develop his own physical abilities. As children practice movement tasks, their brains' connections gradually become more permanent. This allows children to become capable of complex movements using both gross- and fine-motor skills. Children's daily schedules should have a balance of quiet and active times. Children shouldn't sit all day, but they also shouldn't run and jump around all day. Interspersed periods that match each child's maturity level allow all children to maintain a rest-movement balance.

Providing activities that fulfill children's physical needs also helps children reach their full cognitive potential. Young children are full of energy. Make sure to provide adequate outlets for physical activity to help children focus on planned learning activities and prevent chaos. Repetition of physical movement puts the skills into muscle memory, allowing children to use their muscles without having to think about how to perform a task. Activities that challenge similar physical skills should be grouped to give practice and maintain interest—children will get bored if they're always doing the same thing. For example, if the goal is to improve the skills needed for writing, activities like painting on a wall with a large brush, erasing the chalkboard, and making circles in the air all use similar muscle groups needed for writing.

TELEVISION AND PHYSICAL DEVELOPMENT IN PRESCHOOLERS

Television watching is usually a passive activity. When watching programs that include a physical component, encourage children to stand and mimic activities on the screen. Programs like *Dora the Explorer*, *Arthur*, and *Blue's Clues* have added a component for child participation. Try to prevent children from sitting with their legs crossed or bent backwards in a "W" formation. This puts stress on the bones and isn't good for growth. Limit television watching and opt for activities that help exercise developing muscles.

LEARNING CENTERS AND PHYSICAL DEVELOPMENT IN PRESCHOOLERS

Preschoolers are active participants in free play and during time in learning areas. They use their entire bodies as they participate in and move from one activity to another. Large muscles are working as children paint at an easel, pour water into a bucket, stack blocks, and put on dress-up clothes. Small muscles are used to explore musical instruments, shape clay, complete puzzles, turn pages of a book, and add pegs to a pegboard. The following are some of the physical skills children practice while playing in interest centers:

- Hand-eye coordination
- Gross-motor skills
- Fine-motor skills
- Balance
- Strength
- Coordination

PHYSICAL ACTIVITY AND CHILDHOOD OBESITY IN PRESCHOOLERS

Many preschool children are sedentary for much of their day and devote little time to moderate or vigorous physical activity (CDC 2011). They spend hours riding in cars and sitting in front of the television. In addition, busy modern families who are short on time may often choose fast-food options that are high in fat and calories for breakfasts, lunches, or dinners. The result is a higher percentage of young children at risk for obesity as well as the early onset of harmful diseases. More young children have diabetes, heart problems, and high cholesterol than in previous generations.

A child's brain consumes twice the energy as an adult brain and uses more calories for energy than an adult (Chugani 2004). Children need both fat and natural sugar in their diets to sustain brain growth. Fruits, vegetables, whole grains, and protein contain essential nutrients. Consumption of junk food should be kept at a minimum. Healthy snacks, plenty of water, and a balance of nutritious foods are necessary for growing children.

Brains need sufficient glucose, oxygen, and water for optimal brain function. Eating foods that contain glucose, such as fruits, increases attention and helps children focus. Just because you think a child is overweight doesn't mean you should eliminate snacks and all foods that contain sugar. Sugar is a natural component of fruits and other whole foods. The brain needs the glucose to perform the multiple tasks necessary for learning. But the added sugars in baked goods and processed foods can add up to a lot of empty calories. One easy fix is to encourage children to drink water or low-fat plain milk instead of juice and sugary drinks and to eat fruit instead of sweet snacks.

Overweight young children should not be put on a diet. Instead, consult a pediatrician, serve healthful foods, and model good nutrition. Children should not be given foods with artificial sweeteners, as these chemicals could have an adverse effect on health. Most of all, get children up and active to help burn calories in a fun way! The problem of obesity among children is due to both unhealthy diets and insufficient physical activity.

Young children often enjoy cooking. Teaching them to chop, stir, and cut refines both large and small muscles and improves hand-eye coordination. And, when children cook their own food, they are more likely to eat it. Connecting the activity with information about nutrition and healthy eating habits teaches children about a healthful lifestyle. Model good nutrition for children and serve healthful foods. This will have a good effect on children's eating habits. Use task-centered talking as the child explores food: "Your crackers are flat and square. They have a salty top. If you lick the top with your tongue, can you taste the salt? Listen to the sound as you take a bite. Do you hear the crunch?"

PRESCHOOL ACTIVITIES

Serve Nutritious Literary Lunches

❯ Serve oatmeal (porridge) with fruit and nuts, if no child has nut allergies. Read *The Story of the Three Bears*.

❯ Eat cottage cheese (curds and whey) with fresh fruit. Recite "Little Miss Muffet."

❯ Sprinkle parmesan cheese and diced vegetables on cooked spaghetti. Read *Strega Nona* by Tomie DePaola.

❯ Cook vegetables and broth to create soup. Read *Growing Vegetable Soup* by Lois Ehlert or *Stone Soup*.

❯ Assemble whole wheat and natural fruit spread sandwiches. Read *Bread and Jam for Frances* by Russell Hoban.

PRESCHOOL ACTIVITIES

Assemble Healthy Snacks with Children

❯ Ants on a log: Spread a six-inch piece of celery with cream cheese or nut butter. Top with raisins or sunflower seeds. Sing, "The Ants Go Marching."

❯ Egg salad: Place a hardboiled egg and a teaspoon of low-fat mayonnaise in a zippered bag. Knead the mixture and spread it on whole wheat or rice crackers.

- Cereal mix: Measure one cup each of rice, corn, and wheat square cereal into a bowl. Add raisins, pretzels, and peanuts as desired. Stir and enjoy!

- Edible art: Spread cream cheese or natural fruit spread on whole wheat bread, pita rounds, or crackers. Decorate with small stick pretzels, chopped dried fruit, banana slices, and nuts

- Veggies and dip: Dip celery sticks, cucumber slices, or broccoli florets into dip or salad dressing placed in a cupcake paper.

- Pizza: Spread pizza sauce on pita bread, half a bagel, or English muffin: sprinkle with diced vegetables and cheese. Bake in toaster oven until the cheese melts.

- Smoothies: Add fresh or frozen fruit, plain yogurt, and ice cubes to a blender. Process until smooth.

- Apple pie: Flatten out a refrigerated biscuit and place in a cupcake pan. Add unsweetened applesauce, sprinkle with cinnamon, and bake according to biscuit directions.

- Fruit turnover: Separate refrigerated crescent rolls. Spread on natural fruit spread, fold over to create a triangle, pinch edges, and bake.

- Edible jewelry: String round cereals with holes. Allow children to eat when finished.

- Shaker pudding: Shake instant pudding and milk in a tightly shut plastic container. Open and enjoy.

- Ice milk: Place low fat milk with vanilla extract or chocolate low-fat milk in a cylindrical container with a tight fitting lid. Fill two-thirds full. Partially fill an empty coffee can with crushed ice and ice cream

salt. Place the container inside and fill to brim with ice and salt. Place the plastic lid on tightly. Seal with masking tape. Roll between children. Scrap down the sides after ten minutes and every five minutes until the milk is frozen. It takes twenty to thirty minutes. Open and enjoy!

❯ Veggies and rice: Children can chop up canned water chestnuts and bamboo shoots. Put on steamed rice and provide chopsticks. Let them sprinkle on soy sauce if desired.

❯ Tacos: Fill hard shell tacos with shredded cheese, lettuce, and tomatoes; then pour on mild sauce. Roll soft tortillas with cheese.

❯ Sandwiches: Spread bread with butter or nut butter and make a sandwich. Use cookie cutters to create interesting shapes.

❯ Fruit salad: Supervise the cutting of fruits or vegetables for a salad. Talk about the smell and taste of the individual items. Discuss where foods are grown.

❯ Applesauce: Cook apples until tender. Cool. Let children crank the handle of an old-fashioned ricer to make applesauce as an adult holds the bowl.

❯ Fruit pizzas: Roll out raw cookie or pie dough. Children add natural jam and sliced fruit and sprinkle with sugar and cinnamon. Bake according to dough directions.

❯ Cereal bites: Lightly brown bite-sized shredded wheat in margarine. Let the children stir. Sprinkle with parmesan cheese. Toss and eat when cool.

❯ Cookies and muffins: Help children measure, add the ingredients, and stir vigorously. Try to keep the group small so no one waits too long for a turn to help. Discuss how heat changes the consistency. Bake according to package directions.

❯ Corn on the cob: Shuck ears of corn. Cook in a microwave or boiling water. Compare the corn kernels to popcorn kernels.

PHYSICAL ACTIVITY AND ACADEMIC LEARNING IN PRESCHOOL

With the pressure on to enhance academics and literacy offerings, many families and child care programs are eliminating or reducing the amount of time children are active both inside and outside. To help boost the amount of time children are up and physically moving, you have to be creative about adding a physical component to a normally sedentary activity.

Exercise increases the number of capillaries in the brain and increases brain mass (Sousa 2006). Exercise increases blood circulation, which results in more oxygen flowing to the brain and, thus, increased learning potential. Physical activity helps the brain release neurotransmitters, which strengthen the brain cell connections and help thinking processes. Movement and physical activities release neurotransmitters in the brain that help elevate mood and make children feel good.

How can you meet the child's physical needs and academic expectations? You can accomplish this by linking academic learning to exercise. Think about how to take sedentary activities and make them physical. Use the following ideas as well as your own to incorporate movement into traditionally sedentary activities and thereby prevent children from sitting for long periods of time.

PRESCHOOL ACTIVITIES

Turn Sedentary Experiences into Physical Experiences

❯ Read *Curious George Flies a Kite* by Margret Rey and H. A. Rey. Make kites from paper plates. Add a string and crepe paper tails. Run and let the kite fly behind.

❯ Read *Franklin and His Friend* by Paulette Bourgeois. Use plastic bats and wiffle balls to play baseball. Use cones to balance the ball for hitting. Help young children run the bases.

- Read *Clifford Gets a Job* by Norman Bridwell. Use imaginative play to create circus acts. Place masking tape on the floor and walk the tightrope. Tumble on mats like acrobats.

- Transform a board game into real-life action. Instead of moving a plastic figure along a path from start to finish, use a sidewalk with the children hopping, jumping, and skipping along the squares. This activity works well with "Candy Land" and "Chutes and Ladders."

- Play "Hop Scotch" to reinforce numbers, colors, or alphabet letters.

- Throw balls or beanbags into boxes or baskets with alphabet letters posted to review beginning, middle, and ending sounds. Let children shout their answers as they run and touch the letter.

- Label several containers with numerals. Have the children throw that number of balls and beanbags into the container. Then have the children jump or hop the answer to the question, "What number comes next?"

- Change games such as "Mother May I" and "Simon Says" to active participation by all.

- Use Hap Palmer's song "Colors in Motion" to stand up and sit down while naming colors. Use movement songs such as "Head, Shoulders, Knees, and Toes" and "Hokey Pokey" to name body parts. Use your creativity to add a rhythmical beat to "Head, Shoulders, Knees, and Toes" and change the body movements.

- Play charades and act out riddles or vocabulary words.

PHYSICAL ACTIVITY WITH PRESCHOOLERS AT GROUP TIME

Often circle time or group activities have children sitting in a circle or on carpet squares. Change your thinking and see how creative you can be in making part of the time active. Physical activities are fun, and the children can focus better when they have a chance to move. Movement can be related to the theme or academic focus of a lesson. If you're reading a story about an animal, the children can act out how the animal moves and then sit for a short period. The children will be excited to jump up each time you call a number or a color. Plan songs that have movement, and intersperse them between sedentary activities.

PRESCHOOL ACTIVITIES

Promote Physical Activity at Group Time

- Have children hop or jump to find five objects that begin with a specific letter or discover two different size chairs in the room.

- Encourage the children to walk around the room and touch a color on a bulletin board or on the clothing of another child when learning to identify colors. Increase the difficulty by asking them to find the color combination of yellow and red.

- Add a song with hand or body movements, such as "Twinkle, Twinkle, Little Star," to the group time. Gallop like horses in "She'll Be Coming 'Round the Mountain," act like the animals in "Old MacDonald Had a Farm," chant the verse after each animal in "Big Cow, Little Cow, Large Cow, Small Cow," and use large arm movements to illustrate the songs.

- Clap out rhythms, swing scarves, sway rhythm ribbons, or march to music to end group time.

- Ask children to walk, hop, or skip onto number mats or number cards. Children shout out a number and then perform that number of steps, hops, or skips.

- Help each child create a pile of a specific number of small blocks and jump over the pile.

- Recite "Jack Be Nimble" and let each child leap over an unlit candlestick.

- Have children pretend to hold a helium balloon while walking on only one color of tile or on a painted line. Pretend to be a rocket taking off from a crouching position.

- Dismiss children from group time using creative movement with familiar songs or games. Pretend to be a train, airplane, or bus. Move like different animals.

- Play "Red Light, Green Light." Sing and move to "Down by the Station."

- Modify "Ring around the Rosie." Instead of falling down, everyone can jump or stand on one foot. Play "A-Tisket, A-Tasket," "Paw Paw Patch," and "Skip to My Lou" and other skipping games.

- Use fingerplays such as "Five Little Pumpkins Sitting on a Fence" and "Here Is the Beehive."

- Crumple newspaper, throw it in the air, and catch it. Throw it at targets. Have two children roll or throw a paper ball back and forth; end with throwing it in the recycling bin.

- Sing "Five Little Ducks" (went out to play) or "Six Little Ducks" (that I once knew). Ask children to walk like ducks while flapping their wings and quacking.

- Allow controlled jumping and rolling with songs such as "Ten in the Bed" and "Five Little Monkeys Jumping on the Bed." Keep children spread apart to prevent accidental injuries.

- Place a mat in the middle of the circle. Ask children to figure out different ways to cross it: walking, crawling, hopping, leaping, or rolling to the other side.

ACTIVE INDOOR PLAY FOR PRESCHOOLERS

It is prudent to provide adequate physical activity outlets for excess energy to help prevent chaos while inside. Bending and stretching are not only physically important; they also serve as a planned release for excess energy. Repetition of physical movements—through a variety activities, if desired—puts skills into muscle memory, allowing children to use their muscles without having to think about how to perform a task. Activities that challenge similar physical skills and muscles can be grouped for practice. For example, marching and walking up and down steps target the same muscles. Thrusting the arms out in front and pulling them back to music uses the same muscles necessary to throw a ball.

It is important to remember that children need a balance between active and quiet activities. Plan accordingly. Try to incorporate a total of two hours of purposeful, active learning in a young child's day. Not only does it help children refocus; it also helps eliminate the wiggles when you want them to be quiet.

PRESCHOOL ACTIVITIES

Support Physical Play Indoors

- Use tumbling mats to teach children tumbling: somersaults, crab walk, cartwheels, hopping, and jumping skills. Eliminate waiting time by having other activities or multiple mats available. Extra supervision is required.

- Add music as children gallop, run, march, hop, and jump. Provide scarves, Hula-Hoops, paper plates, and rhythm ribbons to move creatively to music.

- Create an obstacle course. Use indoor slides, a low balance beam, movable steps, tires, boxes, child-size chairs, and masking tape lines. Allow children to climb over, under, and through as they walk, hop, and jump in a confined space. Keep everyone going the same direction. Play follow the leader!

- Children's exercise tapes and DVDs exist, but you can create your own exercise routine. Try jumping jacks or touching toes. Exercise quickly or in slow motion.

- Use a small, low exercise trampoline to safely jump on.

- Use "Doggy, Doggy, Where's Your Bone?," "Duck, Duck, Goose," and other movement games to encourage running in a confined space.

- Play "Twister," or make your own game by placing colored circles on the floor. Have children touch the colors you call out. Each hand and foot can be on a color.

- Spread glue with a craft stick or squeeze it from a bottle onto a surface. Pick up a variety of items to put into the glue. Use tweezers for a challenge.

- Provide scissors to cut wallpaper books, magazines, or strips of paper. Cut straws and cardboard. Cut out grocery coupons and put them in envelopes to share with families.

- Provide a variety of sizes of pencils, paintbrushes, nontoxic crayons, and markers, and let each child choose the size best suited to his grip. Add rubber stamps with ink pads, staplers, and old-fashioned adding machines and typewriters.

- Add blunt scissors, rolling pins, craft sticks, dull plastic knives, and cookie cutters for cutting out shapes with playdough and clay.

- Provide a variety of floor and table puzzles. Think of creative ways to assemble them that have the children up and moving.

- Place a pulley and rope between two chairs. Teach children how to move small buckets by pulling on the ropes.

- Place a golf ball in a shallow box. Two children can roll the ball back and forth. Add paper the size of the box and a little paint. Roll the ball to create a pattern.

- Help children actively find colors. Walk around the room and touch a color. Find the color on another child's clothing. Find colors using Al Rasso's song "Orange, Orange, Orange" or Hap Palmer's "Colors in Motion."

- Before naptime, lead children in exercises to get their wiggles out as they lie on their individual mats. Have them slowly exercise arms and legs lying on both their backs and their tummies while listening to very soft music.

Support Active Play Outdoors

Some children, even when outside, become sedentary. However, exciting activities will lure them away from benches. Children seek adult attention and play when teachers give attention. Instead of sitting on a bench, get up and talk to children as they climb, swing, or slide. Children will gravitate to the piece of equipment or activity where they will get your attention.

Children should play outside daily. The experience provides an avenue for running around and feeling their bodies in motion. They experience entirely different physical challenges as they climb on structures, swing, or play games in a large unencumbered area. They feel the sun and wind on their skin as they jump or race around. Outside they can ride tricycles as fast as they want and climb high and slide down quickly. Children love the freedom of being able to move their bodies as much as they want in outdoor spaces. They experience joy and exuberance and release stress as they play. As children explore and hike in nearby natural habitats, their senses are aroused. Learning about nature firsthand while challenging their body is an exhilarating experience. Watching ants move dirt or caterpillars eating leaves on a plant is fascinating. With your guidance, they will learn scientific principles, and their curiosity about the world will be heightened as they challenge their physical strength.

PRESCHOOL ACTIVITIES

Support Physical Play Outdoors

- Provide a variety of climbing apparatuses that require the use of all parts of the body. Add moveable elements to change the play.

- Take a large sheet of paper with the children's names and tally the number of times each child goes down the slide or runs around the tree. It's not a contest as much as it is a way to motivate.

- Make up a rhyme using the children's names while they climb, slide, or run. Clap loudly to attract other children to the activity.

- Have children roll a ball around on the equipment. Encourage children to roll it down or up a slide, across a bench or balance beam, up steps of a climbing apparatus, around trees, and all over the play area.

- Count the number of jumps or hops to go from one part of the playground to the next. Challenge the children to use fewer or more jumps or hops on the return trip.

- Hang paper plates from a tree branch just above the children's heads. Encourage the children to jump and touch the plates. Fill spray bottles with water and let them squirt the plates to make them twirl.

- Add squirt bottles, a variety of containers, and scrub brushes to water play. Wash the playground equipment.

- Encourage children to get up and be active in the sandbox.
  - Include child-size garden shovels and hoes so children have to stand while digging.
  - Keep various sizes of buckets, small shovels, sifters, and molds in a toy box outside of the sandbox.
  - Give children spray bottles to wet down the sand and add transportation toys that can travel on top of the wet sand.
  - Place toy stoves outside of the sandbox. Add cooking pans and muffin tins. Children will have to stand and move to "cook" their pies.
  - Bury shells, toy dinosaurs, colored rocks, large marbles, or pennies in the sandbox. Children can dig like archaeologists searching for buried treasures.

- Garden with shovels, hoes, and trowels. Watering with a hose or watering can requires concentration and strength. Picking weeds aids hand-eye coordination.

- Provide large bubble wands with pans of soap, Hula-Hoops, windmills, and kites.

- Use bikes and wagons on a paved path. Helmets are a must for safety! Add a large appliance box for the gas station, drive-in fast-food restaurant, or car repair shop.

- Provide low basketball hoops, soccer balls and goals, kickballs, and footballs. Encourage children to develop baseball skills by using large bats and wiffle balls placed on cones. Allow running and throwing skills to develop without a formal game with rules.

- Go on movement walks with everyone taking baby steps, giant steps, hopping over sidewalk cracks, or jumping with feet together past a tree. Crouch down and walk, walk on tiptoe, or pretend to skate as you proceed.

- Teach children how to jump rope. Tie a jump rope to a pole and hold it just above ground level for beginning jumpers. Design a game of limbo, and help children walk under the rope.

- Fill tubs with water. Add boats or pouring containers.

- Enhance the outdoor area with woodworking. Provide hammers and screwdrivers. Hammer leaves or flowers placed between two pieces of muslin on top of a wooden block. This creates a stain shaped like the leaf or flower. Extra supervision is required.

- Paint cement areas or large boxes. Put large paper on the fence and let children paint. Use standard-sized wall paintbrushes with buckets of water to paint on walls, sidewalks, or play equipment.

- Hide plastic or stuffed animals on the climbers. Challenge children to climb and find them quickly. Count as they look.

- Bring playdough and clay outside with cutting and shaping implements.

- Distribute magnifying glasses for exploration. Put up a tent and pretend to camp. Use pebbles to make a trail. Draw a map of the pebble path with the children. Have a child direct others using the map to get from one end of the path to another. Take turns.

- Go on a hike.

- Use a portable tape, CD, or MP3 player with music for dancing. Bring out rhythm and band instruments for spontaneous parades.

- Make rubbings of the bark of a nearby tree.

- Run a hose in the mud and create a dam using sticks.

- Narrate action like a circus announcer to describe the children as they climb, slide, and run. Perform circus acts.

- Use tennis rackets or plastic bats to hit balls against a wall. Count the number of bounces.

- Bring large blocks outside and encourage children to build with them.

- Bring dress-up clothes, dolls, and doll carriages outside. Add appliance boxes for houses and stores.

- Act out familiar stories and nursery rhymes incorporating the outdoor equipment into the story line.

CLOSING THOUGHTS

Physical development does not occur in a vacuum. It is closely related to emotional development, social development, and intellectual development. If a child cannot perform tasks that other children can, she may feel bad, which will affect her self-esteem. If she cannot do what others in her group are capable of doing, she can't or won't want to participate, which not only generates feelings of failure, but also prevents socializing and interacting with others. Conversely, children with excellent motor agility have confidence, and they experience positive feelings of success when performing activities well. They are eager to participate and can't wait to play with the other children. Other children want to interact with them because of their abilities. Additionally, physical activity increases children's ability to focus when they return to more structured learning.

The hand-eye coordination and fine-motor skills children practice in block building, painting, and doing puzzles help children develop the skills needed for tasks in kindergarten and elementary school. Children will need to have the eye movements necessary for reading and the refined fine-motor musculature required to write. Motor coordination is an important part of intellectual development, which is discussed in the next chapters.

CHAPTER 6

Cognitive and Language Development of Infants and Toddlers

The early years are the learning years. The first five years of life set the tone for acquiring knowledge for the rest of our lives. Just think of what you learned in your first few years that you still know. You can walk, run, skip, and jump. You understand a language and can talk with a vocabulary that includes nouns, verbs, and adjectives. You construct sentences and use acceptable grammar. You identify numerals and know the difference between number quantities. Your knowledge includes scientific principles, such as gravity and evaporation. You know that the sunrise and sunset have reds, oranges, pinks, and purples and that the moon goes through multiple phases. This is lifetime knowledge that was learned during your first five years. As an infant, you didn't know the word "gravity," but you knew that when you let go of an object, it fell. As a toddler, you looked at the changing shape of the moon each night but didn't understand that the rotating earth caused this. Each year, you added information that later education built on, and that education has never ended!

Everything a young child does is a learning experience. Young children do not need to sit down and learn vocabulary words and the proper construction of sentences. They do not need to be drilled on number concepts or scientific facts. Young children learn by doing and experiencing. Learning occurs when their bodies touch and interact with objects in their surrounding environments. This hands-on education brings about lifetime learning that will be an integral part of their knowledge that they never will forget. Infants and toddlers have an inner motivation and an innate curiosity to explore and learn. You can lead them to actively participate in learning each day.

COGNITIVE DEVELOPMENT: THE INFANT AND TODDLER YEARS

During gestation, the brain develops connections between one *neuron*, or nerve cell, and others that perform the same or similar functions. They connect through a tiny space, called a *synapse*, to hundreds of other neurons that must work together in concert. They communicate with chemicals and electrical impulses. Most of these early synaptic connections control life functions such as breathing, digestion, and blood pressure. This network of connections is like a spiderweb with all the fine threads interwoven and going in multiple directions. The synapses between neurons allow the infant to see, cry, hear, and smell. This wiring has prepared each child for life.

A complicated set of interactions between the body (nature) and the environment (nurture) continues building the web of connections in an orderly process after birth. An infant's brain stem and spinal cord are "wired" to sustain life. Even though an infant has millions of neurons in the cerebral cortex, which are constantly changing as a child learns, they are poorly connected. In a burst, the cerebral cortex creates about two million new synapses every second as the infant's senses bring information into the brain (Zero to Three 2011). The infant's brain responds to this information with chemical and electrical impulses that actually change the physical structure of the brain. Every waking moment, learning takes place.

The brain connections made before birth are used to respond to surroundings and to learn. The newborn will quickly learn to identify his mother by the tone of her voice, the sight of her face, and the smell of her body. Research is progressing rapidly and is discovering what infants know and learn. The amount they learn in the first few months is astonishing! Newborns begin to distinguish between objects immediately, and with each encounter they add information about those objects. Give infants an opportunity to experience their surroundings and master everything their hands and minds can manipulate for learning to take place. During the first year, complex connections occur that lead to skills and knowledge, such as crawling, walking, and talking. Newborns sleep the majority of the day, and while they sleep, their brains are working. Like the spider that must constantly check and repair its web, our brain

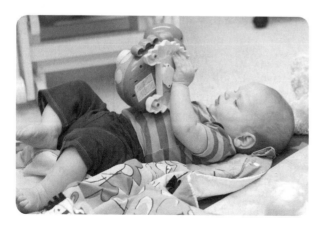

reinforces synaptic connections during sleep. Because everything is new to infants, they need to sleep a lot to process all the sensory inputs.

A toddler's cerebral cortex contains over a hundred trillion synapses by the time she is two years old. Infants make their first connections as they use sight, hearing, smell, and touch to bring in information. After that, the areas of the brain that involve thinking, learning, and emotional functions are wired. This extraordinary explosion of connections continues throughout the preschool years before slowing down as the child matures (Zero to Three 2011).

By age three, each neuron has formed around 10,000 connections. That amounts to around a quadrillion (1,000,000,000,000,000) synapses in the brain, which is twice the number in an adult brain; the web of connections is very dense. After toddlerhood, synapse formation slows, and many connections are pruned over time. That is, the brain removes synapses that are not being used to make room for new synapses to form (MacDonald 2007). This allows us to continue to learn our entire lives.

THE CAREGIVER'S ROLE

Children's caregivers foster learning by providing a rich, experience-based atmosphere. It is important that the caregiver, whether a parent or an early childhood professional, treats children differently at each stage of their development. Adults should add to the environment as the child grows so that the necessary brain connections continue to be made. The caregiver meets the physical needs of the very young infant, who is totally dependent on a trusted adult. The infant's daily schedule is his curriculum (Lally 1998).

The caregiver is the voice of the infant. As described earlier, even though the infant doesn't understand language yet, it is important that she hear meaningful language. A running description of what the infant sees, hears, tastes, and feels as she is fed, diapered, rocked, or moved is called *task-centered talking*. By three months of age, infants are copying the phonemes they hear in the language surrounding them. They begin imitating the vowels and later the consonants in their native tongue long before understanding takes place.

Once mobile, the infant needs to feel secure to explore his world. He is less dependent on the adult to bring the environment to him but instead needs variation in the surroundings. Older toddlers can manipulate the environment by picking up, tasting, and experimenting with objects. As the child's interests lead away from the caring adult, he tries to control objects in his reach. Adults need to support the exploration, encourage manipulation, and help the infant at any stage learn in an environment that is predictable and comforting (Lally 1998).

The impact of a new experience is much greater for young infants. When an infant goes to a park, learning takes place at a faster rate than for an older child or adult who has been to parks many times. The more complex the environment is, the greater the number of connections made between neurons, and the faster the learning occurs and with greater meaning (Sousa 2006). At the park, the infant is bombarded by sunlight and shade and sounds of dogs barking and children playing. She can smell newly mown grass and food from the picnic and see a variety of colors and shapes. She feels the wind on her face and the warmth from the sun. As the senses are excited, brain connections are occurring at a very rapid rate. First experiences often leave indelible memories. As adults, we still

enjoy and relate to the park experience because our brains are pulling up memories and reinforcing existing brain connections. However, our brains are not rapidly creating and pruning connections like children's brains. Children learn best when experiencing things that are novel. The brain discerns things that are new and focuses on the differences. A rich environment stimulates multiple networks in the brain, leading to learning (Perry 2006).

Rich experiences in the first years of life can account for a 20 to 30 percent increase in the number of glial cells, the number of synapses, and thus, brain size and function (Maria 2001). Infants need to experience touching, holding, rocking, talking, listening, reading, and playing. Early experiences build pathways in the brain that influence later social, emotional, language, and intellectual functioning. There is a strong connection between how infants and toddlers feel and how well they learn. Even though children's brains are wired to learn at birth, learning from their surroundings cannot occur unless the children are attached to people they can trust and they feel safe and secure (Lally 1998).

Cognitive Environments

Setting up an environment that is ideal for infants and toddlers to explore and investigate is

imperative. Children have a rich potential to learn from birth, so the area must be geared to provide everything the infants and toddlers need. Safety is paramount. Infant and toddler furniture should be small so they can easily sit and play. Climbing equipment should be low. All toys need to be too big to swallow and must not have small parts that could come off. Be sure there are no sharp objects and the area is kept neat and clean. The room should be warm with colorful toys geared to the infant's developmental age. The primary tool necessary is the nurturing adult and the interaction between the infant and the adult. When the infant is awake, being fed, bathed, and diapered, the caregiver talks and sings as the infant gazes at her face. If the infant is lying on a blanket, the caregiver provides materials to interact with and talks with the infant about the items.

Infants are sitting up by four to five months and are able to reach for and grab blocks and toys to manipulate. Very young children who are able to freely move and engage in play with a variety of objects have more honed networks in the brain. Therefore, it's easy to make the connection that play helps build children's brains. Play should be a major component of the curriculum. And both the curriculum and routines need to revolve around an infant's schedule. Play is how very young children interact and learn in their environments. Children are constructing new knowledge when, through experimentation, they stack graduated rings onto a spindle for the first time. Once they know how to do it, they will repeat the action, practicing what they have learned. They use their senses and practice using their muscles. Every experience becomes a learning opportunity. Sleeping, eating, and diapering consume much of the day. The older the infant is, the longer are the periods of wakefulness. Please remember, every child has his own developmental timetable, and one infant's achievements can't be compared to another's. If in doubt, consult developmental charts.

Once infants are mobile, they can move around to investigate items in the room. Keep the areas simple yet intriguing. Store toys where children can crawl and pick them up on their own. Don't overwhelm them with too many supplies. In group care, have multiples of the same toy. After the children are walking, more toys can be added into the environment.

Change activities often to accommodate young children's short periods of concentration and distractibility. A child can pick up a toy, explore it, taste it, and be ready to investigate something different in a matter of seconds. Keeping the classroom or play space organized and safe is important. Toys have to be constantly picked up and exchanged.

Ratios and group size in child care centers affect brain development. In infant and toddler care, too many children per adult results in only physical needs being met. Some state licensing regulations allow too many children per adult. Infants need at least one adult for every three or four infants under the age of twelve months and a group size capped at six infants. Toddlers need at least one adult for every four to six toddlers from twelve to twenty-four months of age, with a group size of eight to twelve. Two-years-olds need to have at least one adult for every four to six children and no more than twelve in the group (NAEYC 2008). One adult with eleven two-year-old children cannot possibly give the sufficient individual attention that is needed for children to reach their full potential. There is no way they can change diapers, wipe noses, see to the safety of each child, and give the ongoing language description and sensory input necessary to help young minds expand.

Pretend Play with Older Infants and Toddlers

The dramatic play area has an array of items for children to explore while they try to make sense of their world. Recreating a child-size kitchen, bedroom, or living room allows the mobile infant or curious toddler to touch, manipulate, taste, and explore items such as a toy stove or toy car. This pretend area is a re-creation of their world. They are practicing what they have learned in other settings. They learned to put food from a bowl into their mouths during mealtime. In the pretend area of their classroom, they can simulate eating by using toy food and toy utensils, or they can turn a cooking pot into a drum. Children's play is their daily work. You are there to support and facilitate the play. You lend language to the actions of the children and lay a foundation the children will need as they grow older. The following are suggestions for including supplies that promote pretend play with older infants and toddlers:

- Provide small furniture, such as a table and chairs, a toy refrigerator, a stove and sink, a washing machine, and a cabinet to hold supplies.

- Provide child-size nonbreakable dishes, tableware, pots, and pans with lids. Infants and toddlers are drawn to eating implements.

- Include toy fruits, vegetables, meats, and breads. Children quickly learn to pretend to eat, so be sure all items are too large to be swallowed.

- Have small dolls made of a variety of materials that children can easily carry around. Dolls should represent multiple ethnic backgrounds. Also have doll beds, doll strollers, and baby blankets.

- Offer stuffed animals of various sizes.

- Have a supply of shoes, briefcases, and purses of all colors and sizes as well as a variety of hats, caps, scarves, and accessories.

- Place colorful posters of babies, children, and family groups at eye level.

- Provide brooms, mops, and dustpans that are sized for toddlers.

- Include toy telephones, cash registers, and doctor kits.

- Have baskets and containers that can hold objects.

- Incorporate a variety of push toys as well as a variety of pull toys and a small wagon.

- Bring in buckets and boxes of all sizes for children to fill and dump.

- Offer board, plastic, and cloth books of varying sizes and shapes.

Block Play

Blocks are appealing to children of all ages. Infants and toddlers like to pick them up, put them in their mouths, and manipulate them. This play helps young children develop their beginning coordination skills. They start to understand one-to-one correspondence (matching numbers to objects or objects to objects) and object permanence (understanding that something exists even when it can't be seen). When they try to stack blocks, they find that gravity affects their play. They enjoy knocking down a pile of blocks as much as building it up. Through trial and error, they learn that the blocks must be stacked carefully with the weight and size equally balanced on the one underneath. In time a tower is built. This is the beginning of mathematical understanding and a foundation for later mathematical knowledge. The children explore spatial relationships as they place one block next to another and form a rudimentary understanding of shapes.

You are the facilitator. Although the children learn from self-experimentation, you are the catalyst that provides the vocabulary and the challenges that help children acquire knowledge. Children should be initiating the play, but you can contribute expansion ideas. In toddler classrooms, make signs to label creations, suggest additions for the creation, and provide props to expand the play. When a child builds an apartment building, you might suggest building a parking garage and adding a toy car. This not only reinforces knowledge the child has but also helps the child to create a fantasy world from her block creation. The following are suggestions for incorporating supplies for block play with older infants and toddlers:

- Offer large cardboard, foam, or plastic blocks.

- Have smaller natural or colored wooden blocks (too large to swallow).

- Supply unit blocks. Keep the quantity small and the variety of shapes basic.

- Include large cars, trains, buses, and trucks.

- Use props such as toy animals, trees, fences, signs, and people.

- Incorporate large bristle and magnetic blocks that are easy to manipulate and assemble.

- Provide buckets and containers for filling and dumping.

- Once in a while, include items such as cardboard boxes, paper towel tubes, chairs, benches, and large pieces of fabric to spark toddlers' creativity and change the pattern of building and thinking.

- Have a hammering bench or large foam pieces, golf tees, and children's hammers for toddlers and young three-year-olds to begin woodworking.

Manipulative Play

Manipulative play is the avenue for children to refine their fine-motor skills and learn how objects are interrelated. Infants and toddlers use their hands, fingers, and arms to pick up and manipulate objects. The materials encourage the children to gain control of their fine-motor movements. Infants begin with grasping objects, dropping objects, and eventually throwing objects. Young children learn that they can make something happen when they pick up a toy or move it from one place to another. It is exciting, and they want to repeat the action over and over to see if the outcome is always the same. These toys increase their knowledge and do so through the action of the child. Through trial and error, the children begin to problem solve. They learn new skills and reinforce other skills while playing. Coordination and skills learned with one toy are transferred and applied to another toy. These very young children are building a rudimentary knowledge of mathematics, science, and language concepts that accompany each toy.

The adult not only provides the toys but also must match the toy to the child's developmental level to eliminate frustration. The child should be

able to use the material with a little trial and error. The child should be able to succeed and be willing to continue to explore. Once the child can easily do the task, introduce the next level, helping the child build a foundation of knowledge. All the while, narrate the child's actions, describe the colors and shapes, and offer advice on the manipulation of the object so the child can succeed. It is important to extend the children's thinking and understanding as they play. The following are suggested supplies for encouraging manipulative play with older infants and toddlers. Make sure all objects are too large to swallow:

- Supply large wooden one-, two-, and three-piece puzzles, with and without knobs.

- Have large beads and short cords to string.

- Include shape boxes with blocks that fit into triangle, round, and rectangular holes.

- Place on a table a variety of small colorful blocks and sets with interlocking objects specifically made for infants and toddlers.

- Hang a large pegboards with pegs.

- Have nesting cups and graduated stacking rings.

- Attach zippers, buckles, buttons and buttonholes, lacing grommets, and large screws and nuts to a board or sew them onto fabric for fine-motor practice.

Discovery or Science Play

Learning about the world and how to interact in it is an important part of knowledge. Infants and toddlers need a chance to explore both indoors and outdoors. Young children learn best when they can touch and hold something, using all their senses to discover the object's properties. Watching a bug crawl over a flower under a magnifying glass isn't just fascinating, it also opens a whole new area of discovery for children. They can touch a green leaf and a dead leaf as you talk about the color, the feel, and the smell. They can see a picture of the same two leaves in a book and can begin to understand the relationship between real objects and a picture. They hear the descriptive words and build a cognitive foundation that will inform them when they see green leaves in the tree and dead leaves on the ground. Learning about the world around them is very powerful and has meaning. Help children observe what is around them, and encourage them to investigate the details and ask questions. Math is used in scientific exploration as children measure, count, and compare things. Provide the words and mathematical content as children use their senses to explore. Create the learning moments for children to discover. The following are suggestions for incorporating supplies for discovery play with older infants and toddlers:

- Cultivate nontoxic plants and fresh flowers.

- Maintain a fish tank or small animal cages. (Make sure little hands cannot get in!)

- Display colorful posters of the sky, nature, animals, and oceans.

- Provide pouring and measuring cups for the water and sand table, and sponges, hand mixers, and nonstinging soap for water play.

- Bring in fresh fruits and vegetables for children to see, feel, and smell.

- Collect large rocks and shells.

- Supply nature books.

- Have a large magnifying glass on a stand.

Art Area Supplies for Older Infants and Toddlers

For infants and toddlers, art is an exploratory process. Don't expect a clean process or a perfect end result. Very young children go through predictable stages, with the first being an investigation of the materials. When infants or toddlers, who are only in a manipulative stage, are given crayons or paintbrushes, it is a purely kinesthetic experience. They are fascinated that marks suddenly appear. They aren't purposely drawing or painting but are merely finding out how to move the object that creates a mark. As they mature, toddlers learn to make purposeful marks that are a form of scribbling. At first it is uncontrolled scribbling where the child makes one continuous scratch. As he gains better command of the muscles that clutch and guide the implement, he moves into the stage of controlled scribbling. Most toddlers remain in either uncontrolled or controlled scribbling whether using crayons, markers, or paint. Some toddlers move into the next state of named scribble. To you it is just a scribbled blob, but the artist calls it a dog or Mommy.

The child learns to focus and to concentrate as she scribbles. She begins using her imagination and creativity as she explores different mediums. Provide a varying art experience for the child each day. It is the process, not the end product, that guides the selection of materials. There are many different ways to paint and different surfaces to paint on. Every day, children should have the option to paint, to manipulate a sculpting mixture—such as playdough or clay—and to access appropriate crayons, markers, scissors, and paper depending on their age. You provide the information that transforms the clammy feel of playdough or the hard surface of a crayon into a learning experience. You can make suggestions to extend the learning and encourage children to try additional forms of media or different techniques. Once again, task-centered talking takes the activity from exploration into a cognitive experience with interesting vocabulary and concepts. The following are suggestions for including supplies for art play with older infants and toddlers:

- Provide large nontoxic markers, crayons, and pencils and large pieces of paper.

- Have nontoxic playdough.

- Offer low easels with washable paint in non-drip dispensers and large brushes.

- Supply safety scissors with thin strips of stiff paper for easy success (toddlers only).

- Collect paper to tear and recycled envelopes to put the scraps in.

- Have nontoxic glue and a multitude of colorful items (too large to swallow) to paste.

Language Acquisition

There is a genetic predisposition for people to learn to talk. Infants' first form of communication is through cries. Parents and caregivers can learn to distinguish different types of cries to help care for the infant. Hunger, wet diapers, tired, and upset cries are all different. Infants also communicate with smiles. They coo and gurgle and play with vowels and consonants in repetitive, singsong vocalization. In the beginning, their babbling encompasses all the sounds of a variety of languages, but this is refined around three months of age by listening to people talking around them. Infants pick up the intonations of adult speech and begin to recognize the melody of spoken language. They pick up tones as adults talk and begin to understand the emotions expressed in conversation (Caron, Caron, and MacLean 1988). As the infant focuses on your face, echo the infant and repeat the coos and babbles. When you reply to the child's babbles, he is encouraged to stay in this conversation with you. He will stop to listen to your next comment. Infants listen for familiar patterns as you care for them. They begin to recognize the sounds of words that are connected to daily activities such as feeding and diapering. Simplified language that is directed at infants is paramount to their understanding of what is being said.

Infants develop a *receptive vocabulary*, which means they understand what the word or phrase means in the context of what is happening around them. Using infant-directed speech, or parentese, that has a singsong quality attracts their interest in what you are saying. Infants hear the phonemes or individual sounds in our language. Placing the important word at the end of a short sentence seems to be most productive in helping infants gain understanding of what you are saying: "This is oatmeal. You are eating oatmeal." Repeating the same phrase increases their attention. Infants listen for what they expect will be said to them during the conversation around daily activities, such as diapering and feeding. They try to babble the same sounds they hear, which leads to spoken language. Eventually they put the sounds together to create words.

Toddlers understand many of the words that are spoken to them, and they try to repeat words. They learn new words at a rapid pace. Young toddlers can understand and follow simple directions: "Touch your nose." "Turn around." "Wave bye-bye." This happens before they have *expressive language*, or the ability to say the words. They may truncate the phrase "What is that?" to "dat," but the sound along with pointing to an object gives complete meaning to the phrase.

It is imperative that adults talk often to infants and toddlers. The amount of conversation that young children hear and the variety of words you use make a difference in how verbal the child becomes. Using more descriptive language and more complex vocabulary means better literacy for the child. The number of words you speak to a child is also important. Although all adults speak to very young children, using running descriptions and task-centered talking—rather than just short bursts of language—increases a child's exposure to language by thousands of words per day. This adds up to millions of words over the course of the first three years, which positively affects reading and scholastic achievement. The infant and toddler years lay the foundation for later verbal fluency.

Connecting new words to known words helps toddlers learn the new word. Once they understand "ball," then they can learn big, small, red, round, and other ball attributes. When an adult or older child can clarify, identify, and explain what is happening, young children can expand their vocabulary and create brain connections. Task-centered talking lends meaning and sense and helps infants focus and remember the activity (Sousa 2008). To extend the learning taking place, add a commentary that clarifies what the child has just discovered. Narrate what has occurred: "You are looking at the ball. It's moving fast as it rolls across the green grass." "You ran to Mommy!"

Often when babies are babbling, a parent hears, "Dada," and gets excited and says, "You said, Dada! Yes, I am Dada!" even though it was just a string of vowels and consonants. The parent's excitement is the infant's reward for repeating it. As caregivers reinforce the babbling, meaning is connected to the sounds. Soon a child will say her first word. Usually the word has one or two syllables and categorizes things (such as "dog" or "book"). By categorizing things in the environment, the child's brain begins to build connections between the thing itself and the word that is used to describe it. Now when the child purposefully says "Dada," or "Mama," she is not just saying a collection of sounds but is expressing a word that she understands means "mother" or "father." The word may only be recognizable to the parent or caregiver. Sometimes very young children associate a babbling sound or tongue thrust with a specific word and repeat it when seeing the object. Again, an animated response from an adult reinforces the repetition of the word or sound.

The age that a child says his first word varies greatly within the normal range. It depends on a variety of things: the amount of conversation in his environment, and physical maturation of the mouth, lips, and tongue muscles, along with the coordination of the vocal cords. Imagine how complex spoken language is as the muscles in the tongue and lips move, and the lungs regulate the breath to move the vocal chords. The child has to coordinate the physical motions with the thought process to produce the spoken word! Infants and toddlers begin pointing to objects and often parrot simple words or the last word of a sentence as the caregiver labels objects. This leads to further muscle practice and coordination that eventually

results in spoken language. Encourage families to consult their pediatrician if they have concerns about an infant's or toddler's response to sounds or their lack of language acquisition.

Flash cards or other products that supposedly teach infants to read are a sales gimmick that should be avoided. Without making sense or having meaning, infants and toddlers do not learn to read with comprehension (Sousa 2006). Instead, spend your time reading a book to the child.

INFANT & TODDLER ACTIVITIES

Foster Language Development

> Read to children from infancy. Hearing spoken words in conjunction with seeing pictures helps language development. The warmth and soothing feeling of sitting on a lap helps create a love of reading. As long as infants are interested in the activity, read to them. Many like to carry around a favorite book.

- Read short, simple picture books to infants often during the day.

  - Point out pictures and use one or two descriptive words.

  - Stop the moment the child loses interest.

  - Let the child hold and even taste the book (plastic, cloth, or cardboard books).

  - Help turn the book so the child sees it right side up.

  - Read books with lots of vocal animation and expression. Use varied pitches and tones as you read.

  - Act out the story or pictures. Pretend to smell the flower or taste the food as you describe the action.

- Make your own picture books. Place two photos back-to-back into page protectors. Connect three or four pages together with yarn or ribbon to create a photo album for the child to hold and view. Change the photographs often.

- Recite nursery rhymes and fingerplays while wiggling the child's fingers and toes and using dramatic tones.

- Slow down and repeat two or three key words of each sentence to help the child understand. Use the parentese singsong to draw the child's attention to the words.

- Play games like "This Little Piggy," "Open, Shut Them," and "Where's the Baby?" to spark a "conversation" with the child.

- Take a trip to the zoo or aquarium; this fascinates infants and toddlers. They sit in the stroller and look intently or point to animals they see. This is a time to name the animal and use task-centered talking to give the young child information about the animal. Keep it short and simple. Add the sound the animal makes.

- Sing to children using a wide range of sounds. Don't worry if you sound off key. As long as the infant is interested, that is all that matters.

- Repeat the infant's coos and babble as if you are creating an echo using her pitch and tone.

- Smile and show joy in hearing the infant vocalize.

- Use correct pronunciation and grammar, but don't correct children. When infants and toddlers begin to talk, they often leave off the ends of words or can't produce all the consonants. Most will self-correct if left alone. It is important not to mimic them or use "baby talk."

- Use baby sign language to alleviate a preverbal child's frustration at not being able to communicate with others. Consult specialists and books to learn the techniques.

- Ignore stuttering. Toddlers have a hard time getting the words out and stutter. Their thoughts are moving faster than their ability to coordinate their mouth, lips, and tongue. Don't correct or call attention to it. This is a stage many children go through that will disappear with maturation.

Writing

Children as young as eight months of age pick up and try to write with the implements they see adults using. Watching the people in their environments informs very young children. They model and copy what they see around them. It is important that older infants and young toddlers see adults writing in a variety of instances. Picking up a rattle or pulling a lever on a toy are examples of fundamental practice in small-muscle control of hands and fingers. Young children learn to grasp objects and let them go. Fine-motor and hand-eye coordination skills are slowly developing. Soon they pick up an object that makes a mark. Just as children go through the early stages of art, young toddlers begin writing as a kinesthetic exercise. It is fun to move the crayon, marker, or pencil, and they become fascinated with the marks it makes. This is the first step to literacy!

Keep the writing implements for young toddlers large and provide supervision to prevent injuries. Have a variety of textures and sizes of paper within easy reach and have nontoxic markers, crayons, chalk, and pencils available. Let children see adults writing often. Toddlers and two-year-olds might scribble and name the picture. That is the perfect time to step in and write the word for the child. Be sure to ask permission before writing directly on a child's picture. With your help, very young children can send a card to a relative or make a note for a family member or friend. Just writing the child's name on a blank piece of paper before he begins using an implement allows him to see the formation of the letters of his name. Make sure you are on the child's level, and place the paper in front of him so that he sees you writing his name from the proper perspective.

Many play activities help develop the muscles used in writing and increase hand-eye coordination:

- Painting with a variety of implements and fingerpainting

- Placing items (too large to swallow) into glue

- Manipulating playdough

- Cutting and tearing paper

- Working puzzles and pegboards, stringing beads

- Using utensils to eat

- Reciting fingerplays and clapping hands

- Throwing beanbags and balls at targets

- Moving pieces on a path while playing board games such as "Candy Land" (Don't worry about winning or losing, just have fun!)

- Fitting shapes into holes

- Building with blocks

- Playing musical and rhythm instruments

- Pouring water and filling sand buckets

Intellectual Development of Mathematics

Infants are born with a genetic predisposition to learn numbers. They have an inborn "number sense" that allows them to compare groups of objects and to be able to see differences. Infants

can recognize up to three objects just by sight. They can detect a difference between one, two, and three items (Sousa 2008). Counting is necessary to identify differences in groups of objects of four or more. Young toddlers discover numbers and soon learn there are number words to compare and measure quantities. Most toddlers have heard people counting multiple times and understand the concept of counting. They begin to count using the words they have learned; however, in the beginning it is common for children to skip a number or recite them in random order. This is very normal. Rather than correcting the child and saying she is wrong, model the correct way to count. Children can learn to count by rote memorization but often don't understand the concept. Give them many concrete experiences with counting small quantities. This will help them associate the word with the quantity.

Create age-appropriate and meaningful events where children can be actively involved in learning math vocabulary and number sense. Mentioning the number of oranges in the bag, the shape of the moon, or the measurement of flour in cookie dough brings mathematics into the child's world. Reading books that count animals and objects or have characters added to the plot draws attention to numbers. The child is given two pennies or two jellybeans, and he wears two shoes. After seeing multiples of many items and hearing the word over and over, he learns that when he sees a group of two items, the word "two" applies to them. Later the numeral will be connected to the word. The material is learned over time. When the number makes sense and is meaningful, then the information is moved into working memory (Sousa 2006).

More is one of the first quantities understood. This is not a direct quantity but is used in many instances, from offering food to offering toys or books. It is probably learned easily because it is ingrained into the child's life from early infancy. Later, the child learns to quantify. Infuse mathematical concepts into daily activities like snacktime: "You took three crackers and three pretzels from the basket for your snack." Toddlers are learning that numbers are associated with counting and that they can use them in language. As they begin using numerical words, they don't know exactly the quantity that the words represent. One-to-one correspondence is a skill they will learn with experience.

INFANT & TODDLER ACTIVITIES

Support Math Skills

❯ Count with infants and toddlers as you use task-centered talking: "I am washing your two hands. First this one. Now the second one." "Here are your two red socks, one for this foot and one for that foot. Now you have on two socks."

❯ Recite nursery rhymes and fingerplays with numbers.

❯ Use number words and quantities as food is placed on the plate or table. Keep the quantities small so the child can see the group of food items: "Here are three slices of banana."

❯ Count objects in picture books as you read: "Here is one duck and one fish and one tiny frog."

❯ Make a game of counting fingers and toes after diapering or dressing.

❯ Play a simplified version of "I Spy" where you talk for the child. Look for small numbers of objects in the child's vision: "I see two balls. Let's go across the room and find them. Here they are: one ball, two balls. You found two balls!"

❯ Point out the shapes as the child plays with blocks or strings beads. Remark on the shape of a book, an egg, or a ball. Identify objects in his world that are shapes, such as the rectangular seat of a swing or the roundness of a spoon.

❯ Use quantitative words as you prepare a food or serve it to the child. Talk about half of a cookie and a whole apple. Compare quantities using the words "more" or "less." Talk using measurement vocabulary, such as cup, teaspoon, and gallon, as you prepare and serve food.

❯ Sing songs with numbers.

Circle Time

Mobile infants and young toddlers are up and about exploring, so the group instruction typically used in preschool settings isn't very practical. In groups of mobile infants and young toddlers, it's better to sit on the floor with a fascinating toy or book, invite children to come over, and allow them to come and go as they like. Infants and young toddlers should not be expected to sit still in a group. Not until a child can sit and attend to a topic without distraction will group time become viable. Each child differs. Some are ready for a five-minute group at eighteen months. Others can't sit still until three or four years of age. When inviting older toddlers to an organized group time, allow them to wander away from the group and do something else. This prevents a struggle. Keep group time short. You want it to end before the children get tired of doing it. Try to keep it under ten minutes, and plan on three completely different topics and a balance of active and passive activities. As suggested in the activity ideas that follow, math and music activities lend themselves to group time with older toddlers.

Promote Cognitive and Language Development at Group Time

❯ Read a story with lots of pictures. Keep the wording very simple and act out the story with your voice. You do not have to read every word. Give each character a different pitch and tempo. Your vocal animation will attract young children and keep them interested.

❯ Pass around one stuffed animal. Teach the children the sound the animal makes. Children then make the same animal sound during their turn to hold the toy.

❯ Clap out a simple pattern. Have the children repeat the pattern. Gradually make it more difficult. Stamp the pattern with your feet.

❯ Recite fingerplays with the group. They can imitate the movement as you say the words. Act out simple fingerplays so every child is participating. "Five Little Monkeys Jumping on the Bed" can be changed to accommodate the number of participating children.

❯ Play "Follow the Leader" as you move about the room. Add different arm movements or different size steps, or repeat a pattern as you jump and hop.

❯ Jump, march in place, bend, and stretch. Do exercises.

❯ Pass a beanbag around the circle. When it stops, the child with the beanbag throws it into a bucket.

❯ Give each child a large piece of paper. Let the children tear the paper and put the scraps in a pile on a sheet. Jump into the pile. Put the scraps into an empty water table. Provide shovels, spoons, and buckets for the children to scoop them up.

❯ Tape together large pieces of paper to form a paper rug. The children sit facing the paper. Give each child a nontoxic crayon or marker to create a class mural.

❯ Put one shoe from each child in the center of the circle. Let a child pick someone else's shoe and give it to the owner. An alternate way would be to pass the shoe around the circle, and when it reaches its owner, she keeps her shoe.

❯ Give each child a truck or car to move, making appropriate sounds. Show pictures of transportation vehicles and repeat the sounds they make.

❯ Talk about the children's clothing. Have them wiggle their shoe. Point to their shirt. Find a pocket, zipper, or button.

❯ Teach children to hold hands, walk in a circle, and shake another child's hand. Hold both hands of a partner and turn in a circle together.

❯ Blow bubbles and let the children pop them. Pop them with hands; pop them with feet, elbows, and knees.

❯ Hide a few toys under a blanket and ask the children what is underneath. For children without language, use task-centered talking as you reveal the hidden objects.

- Show children three objects. Cover them with a blanket and remove one without showing it to them. Uncover the remaining objects and ask what is missing.

- Use a large towel so four to six toddlers can hold on together. Lift it up and down. Walk while holding it. Walk in a circle. Make it go high and then touch the floor.

- Recite nursery rhymes. Act out simple rhymes like "Little Jack Horner" or "Jack and Jill."

- Roll and gently bounce balls as you call out a child's name. Teach them to roll it back to you. Ask them to roll the ball to another child.

- Walk on colored squares and sing color songs. Don't have more than two colors out at a time. When you stop, tell each child what color they are standing on.

Music

Music should be a part of every day for all very young children. Children learn a lot about spoken language and communication through music. Songs have the rhyme, rhythm, and cadence of spoken language. As children mature and develop, listening to music can be augmented with participation. Moving the body to music, singing, humming, acting out parts of the song, clapping, and dancing activate the brain in multiple ways. Dopamine, the "feel-good neurochemical," is released causing emotional reactions of pleasure (Salimpoor et al. 2011).

Learning to appreciate music can't begin too early. Give infants and toddlers the opportunity to listen multiple times during the day to a variety of music types—but remember, don't have music on all day. Children's brains will block out continuous noise. Let them experiment with rattles, toys that make musical sounds, and music boxes. Give toddlers rhythm instruments and toy instruments to explore. They will learn very early that they can perform an action that creates a sound, and that is empowering.

INFANT ACTIVITIES

Support Music Skills

- Expose infants to all forms of music: classical music, folk music, and instrumental music, for example. Play the music for a specific amount of time. Music should start and stop so children pay attention to it.

- Sing as the infant is being diapered, riding in the car, or taking a bath. He doesn't care what you sing or if you're in tune.

- Provide musical mobiles and balls with differing tones. Infants are not just seeing the objects, they are hearing them at the same time.

- Have wind-up music boxes and jack-in-the-boxes. Infants may want you to do this over and over, and you should continue as long as they are interested.

- Sing "Rocking, Rocking in My Rocking Chair" as you rock the baby. Make up a simple tune that you can repeat or piggyback the words onto a simple tune you already know.

- Play soothing music before bedtime. This is a good time to listen to classical music. Be sure to turn the music off so that children can go into deep sleep.

- Put a young child on your knee and sing "This Is the Way the Ladies Ride." Hold the infant and bounce her gently. Repeat with the second verse, "This is the way the gentlemen ride," and bounce a little faster. Then say the child's name in the rhyme and increase the intensity of the bouncing. Use a similar action with "Pop Goes the Weasel" or "Yankee Doodle."

- Sit and touch different body parts for the infant as you sing "Hokey Pokey."

- Stop and sing songs about animals when you are reading a book with pictures of those animals.

- "Mary Had a Little Lamb," "Baa, Baa, Black Sheep," or "Three Blind Mice" are simple, short songs to insert into reading a picture book.

- Show young children how to hit drums with their hands or shake tambourines. Help them experiment with creating sounds.

TODDLER ACTIVITIES

Support Music Skills

- Create a very simple drum song with one or two strikes on a drum. Teach the toddler to recreate the pattern. Create a give-and-take game where both the adult and the child originate the pattern. Repeat with clapping, a tambourine, a triangle, a wood block, and other rhythm instruments. Each child should have an instrument to try to imitate the pattern in a small group.

- Sing along with music. Use chart paper to write and illustrate the song.

- Have child-size musical instruments such as drums, bells, keyboards, xylophones, and triangles available for exploration. Recognize attempts at creating music.

- Play a rhythm instrument that the children can't see. Place several instruments in front of them and see if they can identify which one made the sound.

- Help children imitate tunes and songs they know. "Row, Row, Row Your Boat," "Twinkle, Twinkle, Little Star," and "Old MacDonald Had a Farm" are easy tunes for beginners. Add body movements to include more senses. Hum the tune and let them guess what song it is.

- Have children shut their eyes as they listen to music. What do they imagine while they listen?

- Clap to the beat of a favorite song.

- Point out different instruments, such as a drum or a horn, while listening to classical music. Have the featured instrument or a photograph of it available.

- Walk or crawl to different rhythms of music: walk fast, walk slow; crawl very fast, crawl very slow; bend, sway, jump, and twirl to the music. Move to different tempos of music, march to different rhythms around a small area, and add rhythm instruments.

- Wave scarves, ribbons, or paper plates or clap to the beat of music. Each child should have an item.

- Give each child an empty paper towel roll to use as a horn. March.

- Sing songs children know. Stand up and repeat them with whole body action.

- Clap hands and sing, "This is the way we clap our hands." Crawl while singing "Inchworm."

- Play freeze dance. March or walk around to music. When the music stops, the children freeze or sit down.

- Follow the directions of simple creative movement songs. Some favorites are "Head, Shoulders, Knees, and Toes," "Bend and Stretch, Reach for the Sky," or "Hokey Pokey." Slow down the song for toddlers.

- Encourage children to create their own dance movements to various types of music.

- Use music as transitions to let children know it is time to change activities or go outside. Make up little tunes for daily activities: "This is the way we clean up, clean up, clean up."

- Teach fun songs with lots of finger action: "Little Bunny Foo Foo," "If You're Happy and You Know It," and "Put Your Finger in the Air."

- Use "All the Fish" by Jackie Silberg to illustrate big and little with both voice pitch and volume plus arm movements. Change it to other creatures that live in water.

- Sing story songs, such as "Baby Beluga" by Raffi, "I'm a Little Teapot," "The Wheels on the Bus," and "Itsy Bitsy Spider" and act out the movements as you sing. Find a book that illustrates the song and show the pictures as you sing.

- Sing "The Muffin Man" before eating muffins or "On Top of Spaghetti" before or after eating meatballs or spaghetti.

- Sing "Twinkle, Twinkle, Little Star" using flashlights instead of stars. Give each child an easy-to-use nonbreakable flashlight to turn on and off while singing.

- Hum the tune or sing "la, la" to songs instead of using words.

- Make up new verses to songs that use actions. "The People on the Bus" could hop on one foot, jump up and down, or shake a friend's hand.

CLOSING THOUGHTS

Infants and toddlers are learning machines. They are learning every second they are awake, and the experiences they have and the language they hear structure their cognitive development. Their brains are especially active, and they need the best teachers and an engaging environment to ensure that they go through the necessary steps to prepare them for the next stage of learning. Adults are key to this development. By setting up appropriate interactive environments that are both nurturing and stimulating, you ensure children's success. Infants and toddlers learn as they play. The tending of their physical needs by a caring adult becomes their curriculum. The rich environment, the exposure to a variety of activities, and voices talking, reading, and singing are important components of the child's curriculum. Infants' and toddlers' intellectual growth is closely tied to their physical maturation and their emotional well-being. As they communicate with others and begin to socialize, all domains act together to bring about optimal learning.

Providing an enriching, language-filled environment for infants and toddlers starts them on the path to knowledge. You are helping them create a foundation upon which all other learning will rest. It is like a ladder of information. The first few rungs begin at birth, and the more experiences infants and toddlers have, the higher they can go on the ladder, preparing them for the cognitive challenges they will face later in life.

CHAPTER 7

Cognitive and Language Development of Preschoolers

Giving all children the opportunity to develop critical-thinking skills is the best legacy you can provide. Children who master how to learn on their own will carry this skill with them their entire lives—give them a feeling of success. You don't always have to teach; instead, you can simply allow children to learn. Piaget observed that when children participate actively in a task, they learn. Do hands-on activities make a difference? And if so, what activities are the best to help children reach their genetic intellectual potential? Yes, the child's body needs to interact with real objects for learning to take place. This chapter will describe activity ideas to help children reach their full potential.

Children's basic attitudes toward themselves, learning, and school are established during the early years. When children participate in a developmental, hands-on program, they feel good about themselves, enjoy the learning experience, and will like going to school. Hopefully, they will have a lasting desire to acquire skills and knowledge.

Children possess individual abilities that will help them succeed in the world. Some children excel at math, others learn multiple languages easily, others move with amazing agility, and still others are musically gifted. Howard Gardner's (1983) original theory of multiple intelligences identifies seven human intelligences:

- Linguistic intelligence: Children who possess this intelligence are good at expressing their thoughts and ideas. Much of our education system targets this strength.

- Logical/mathematical intelligence: Children with logical/mathematical intelligence grasp numbers and number concepts easily. They learn to tell time at a young age and can visualize quantities quickly. A lot of time is spent in educational curricula teaching to this strength.

- Musical intelligence: Children begin to move to rhythms and recreate music they hear when they possess this intelligence. They enjoy singing and ask to listen to music. They often can pick out a tune on an instrument without formal instruction.

- Bodily-kinesthetic intelligence: These children are comfortable in their bodies and use gestures and dance moves to express themselves. They have a hard time sitting still and want to touch everything around them.

- Spatial intelligence: Young children with this intelligence are little architects who can build elaborate structures or budding interior decorators who can set up a fantasy world by rearranging the dramatic play area. They can visualize areas. They can follow maps, and their drawings have a three-dimensional quality.

- Intrapersonal intelligence: This intelligence brings about self-esteem that comes from a knowledge of their own abilities. Children with this attribute exude confidence and persevere on difficult tasks. They are resilient and try to master tasks by themselves.

- Interpersonal intelligence: Children with this ability are the social butterflies of the group. They interact easily with others and can see others' points of view. They sympathize and empathize with both children and adults.

Gardner (1999) has since named an eighth intelligence, naturalist, and a ninth potential intelligence, existential:

- Naturalist intelligence: These children are fascinated with nature and enjoy gardening, collecting bugs and leaves. They will watch a caterpillar or butterfly for extremely long periods. They enjoy nature books and seek more knowledge about their world.

- Existential intelligence: This intelligence is the ability to think and question surroundings, including life, death, and reality. Practical chil-

dren who question everything often have this intelligence. They stand back and observe until they thoroughly understand the task; then they participate. They think through problems and try their solutions.

Each child's intelligence is valuable and should be fostered by frequent exposure through activities that support and challenge it. To have a curriculum that truly meets each child's growing needs, you must gear activities to each child's strengths.

COGNITIVE DEVELOPMENT: THE PRESCHOOL YEARS

Just as in infancy and toddlerhood, the senses bring new information into the preschooler's brain. The input causes brain cells to signal other neurons with chemical and electrical impulses. The more that senses are stimulated by an experience, the more interconnected different areas in the brain become from the experience. Having a variety of experiences that engage multiple senses helps to solidify these connections in the brain. Thus, creating a vast, interconnected network helps the child continue to learn and grow from his experiences.

In our modern society, children often suffer from sleep deprivation. This affects both the emotional stability of preschoolers and their ability to focus on learning and storing information. It's important to be responsive to preschoolers' physical needs, including their need for sleep. Encourage families to provide their preschoolers with ten or more hours of sleep a night. And be sure a nap is part of the afternoon routine for children in your care. During sleep, the brain processes information and strengthens connections (Schiller 2010). Sleep helps the child to attune to environmental clues that increase thinking, learning, and memory (Sousa 2006).

Memory is necessary for learning to take place. Unless the information that we want children to know is put into memory, the information is not learned. *Working memory* is the ability to manipulate and use information that is being experienced or presented; it is a temporary form of memory. Sometimes this information is pulled from former memories. For example, when building with blocks, the child pulls stored information about gravity and the need for both a foundation and careful placement of blocks into his working memory. A child sees a doll with tangled hair and remembers how a brush takes knots out of hair. She then moves that information into working memory and finds a brush to use on the doll. We want children to retrieve the information they learn so they can use their knowledge in the world. Memory is important for the acquisition of language, reading, mathematics, and basically everything the child will do.

Repeating meaningful information in the same form can move that information from working memory into long-term memory. This is different from a drill. A drill is recitation without connecting meaning to the activity. Drilling on the alphabet, for example, is futile if it has no meaning for the child. A lapse of repetition in these cases results in the loss of the skill because the material was never truly learned (Sousa 2006). Information must be understood and have a logical connection to the object or action for it to move from working memory to long-term memory. When adults tell children information, children can briefly remember. It takes continuous rehearsal and repetition for the information, such as reciting the presidents of the United States in alphabetical order, to stay in temporary memory. Without total comprehension, the information is not learned and cannot be moved into long-term memory. The connections that form for short-term memories are transient and disappear quickly without constant reinforcement.

When young children participate in their environment and their bodies and minds interact with objects, learning takes place at a rapid rate. Hands-on learning is lifetime learning. Once children learn to ride a bike or swim, they will remember how to do it for the rest of their lives. A rich environment, where children can explore and learn from the activity, allows children to make a great number of brain interconnections. Think of the brain's connections as a fishing net: the more connections you have between the strings, the more likely you are

to catch something. The connections in the brain work in a similar way. The more connections you have between different pieces of sensory information, the more likely you are to retain new information and move it to permanent memory.

By reviewing information while participating in different activities, children will retrieve information from one setting and relate it to another. In that manner, children will learn that the apples they eat, the apples on a tree, and the apples in the grocery store are related to the apples used in applesauce and apple juice. When they hear *The Giving Tree* by Shel Silverstein and the story of Johnny Appleseed, they understand and remember what an apple tastes and looks like. Thus the memory for "apple" becomes complete, but it is enhanced when eating apple cobbler or hearing someone describe candied apples.

Discussing new information helps children to make connections to existing knowledge—that is, it helps them move new information from immediate experience into memory. Asking a child to tell a friend or relative about a recent event or explain a science activity is a form of rehearsal. Use a daily activity that asks children to tell others about their just-completed play. By reviewing the recent actions, children move information from immediate memory to working memory.

Keep in mind, though, that if children repeat the same task over and over in the exact same way, they stop thinking about it and the process becomes automatic. When a child is told to sit and work a puzzle that he has previously mastered, he doesn't have to think about where each piece fits. Instead, he can work the puzzle and think about something else he wants to do. The brain focuses on new, exciting activities but often ignores stimuli that are repeated in the same manner day after day. When this happens, the brain stops paying attention and looks for other, more interesting input (Perry 2003).

Just as reciting numbers or alphabet letters every day in the same way becomes habit, tasks also can become rote. Children can stop thinking and still be able to recite the letters of the alphabet in order or do a common task like hand washing.

Repeating a daily activity such as "the calendar" in the same way allows children to participate in the activity and still think of other things. Impossible? Adults do the same thing. How many times have you driven to work (perhaps while singing with the radio, planning your next activity, and thinking of the upcoming day) without paying much attention to the street-by-street progression between home and work? You traveled from home to work but may not remember much of the details in between. Children can also contribute to a group with something they know, like the color of an object, but be thinking of a previous incident that is emotional. Children can recite memorized fingerplays or nursery rhymes and not have any focus or thought on the activity. Activities must vary to keep the brain engaged. Add or change the environment frequently to provide a challenge. That will keep the brain learning (Perry 2003).

THE CAREGIVER'S ROLE

Teachers and parents need to create an atmosphere that incorporates their scientific knowledge of brain development with their best teaching skills. *Brain-compatible learning* is the result of this application of teaching strategies based on neuroscience (Gregory and Parry 2006). A brain-compatible teacher understands what each child needs at each stage of development and alters the learning environment to meet those needs. Since each child develops by her own timetable, you will need to determine which activities are developmentally correct for each child and when extension activities need to be added for enrichment. The child's brain development dictates the child's needs. Here are attributes of a brain-compatible environment (Gregory and Parry 2006):

- Is safe

- Is varied

- Is stimulating

- Allows for creativity

- Is democratic

- Encourages diverse thinking

- Supports and challenges learning

- Develops relationships

To create a brain-compatible learning environment, teachers have to apply information about how the brain learns to their teaching practices. Young children learn best in an enriched environment that is novel and that provides opportunities for firsthand experiences. A brain-compatible setting allows children to explore materials for long periods while the adult provides support, additional information, and vocabulary. Children need trusting relationships with their teachers and encouragement to take safe risks in a calm, stress-free atmosphere. Expose children to the same information in a variety of ways to keep them engaged. Ask challenging questions and provide just enough assistance to help the children succeed.

The best experiences that bring about the most learning are events that occur naturally. Discussing gravity after a block building collapses or spilled paint drips to the floor brings understanding and meaning to a vague concept. Children could not learn as much from a description of gravity

without seeing it happen. Capture the moment to make teaching real. If that can't occur, then recreating experiences for the children is the next best way to teach. Bring flowers, insects, fruits, animals, plants, and a variety of objects into the learning areas. Help children explore until their curiosity is satiated. Augment experiences with books that delve deep into nature and explain mechanics. This is much better than just trying to teach from books, pictures, and words alone. Symbolic information has the least impact on the brain, as it only involves two senses, seeing and hearing (Jensen 2005). Children need to be immersed in activities that activate all their senses to result in learning that is significant and that helps them understand concepts (Sousa 2008).

To maximize learning, information should be dynamic and stimulate the child's brain to send electrical impulses and release chemicals to strengthen connections and develop new wiring. The following are ways to maximize learning:

- Ensure that the child feels safe taking risks to learn material in a stress-free atmosphere.

- Make the material appealing. The child is then motivated to experience the activity.

- Design the task to appeal to all the child's senses and to introduce new and exciting stimuli.

- Present riveting experiences that are meaningful to children. Meaning is derived when the child interacts with objects.

- Create action-oriented tasks rather than passive activities such as listening to someone describe an event.

These best practices can be accomplished by presenting information in a way that matches the maturity and readiness of the learner. In an optimal developmentally appropriate environment, children are engaged in a variety of activities from playing in sand and water to painting and pasting. Intentionally teach concepts that extend children's thinking and knowledge. Know each individual child, including his strengths and the extent of his knowledge, and use a variety of strategies that lead to learning. Not only do children participate in block play, gardening, pretend play, story time, and a variety of learning centers, but teachers instruct them in a fun, engaging manner so self-discovery is coupled with learning factual information. Teacher-directed instruction is often the bridge children need to learn from experience and to apply the knowledge to their play (Copple and Bredekamp 2009). Age-appropriate activities that children can explore on their own through self-motivation encourage learning. Children are thinking and problem solving as they freely explore their environments (Elkind 2001b). Children learn less than half of the information when a teacher talks and shows cards with colors or numerals and pictures of numbered quantities. They learn most when they manipulate objects.

Support Thinking

‣ Place ice cubes in an electric pan. Watch as they melt. As water becomes steam, hold a mirror over it. Watch as the steam condenses on the mirror and drips back into the pan. Discuss evaporation.

‣ Place a popcorn popper in the middle of a clean sheet on the floor. Help the children establish rules about how everyone should sit around the perimeter of the sheet to prevent burns. Pop popcorn without a lid. Let the children predict what will happen to the kernels as they pop. Use the children's ideas about how to divide the popcorn for all to enjoy.

‣ Bring in two red, two yellow, and two green apples. Cut one of each color into slices and taste them. Ask the children to decide which apple is the juiciest, the sweetest, or the most tart. Count the seeds in each apple. Have the children predict if another apple of

the same color will have the same attributes and the same number of seeds. Cut the apples and discover the answer. This can also be done with red, green, and purple grapes or different species of pears.

Changing the Environment

Changing and enriching the environment not only gives children new experiences but also motivates them to try new activities. The room arrangement remains the same, but a new task is occasionally added to the familiar area to extend learning. Now play becomes new and exciting, stimulating new brain connections to form. Thinking is at its highest level as children approach these activities. Step back and let children create the play atmosphere suggested by the items. You can then move in and add comments that will inform children about what they have just accomplished and add facts that will extend the children's knowledge.

Explore Outdoor Environmental Changes

‣ Camping: Erect a tent in one area of the outdoor play space. Establish a rotational system that gives fifteen minutes of play in the tent to a small group of children. Use a large appliance box as a camper.

‣ Car wash: Use sponges, soapy water, and scrub brushes to clean wagons and tricycles. If possible, once a year bring a real car into the area and let the children have the thrill of washing a car.

‣ Bubble mania: Place a variety of bubble-blowing wands of various sizes throughout the play area. Place the bubble mixture in shallow pans. Provide fly swatters with holes, cans with both ends removed and sanded smooth, plastic six-pack holders, and bent metal hangers.

‣ Decorate the play area: Weave crepe paper into a chain-link fence. Wrap play equipment with thick

yarn, ribbon, and crepe paper. Use washable paint to decorate wooden apparatuses. Take photographs and write a story.

❯ Bike race: Line up tricycles. Have children follow a route. Children ride one at a time. Use a flag and stopwatch. Everyone is a winner!

❯ Cloud shapes: Lie in the grass and gaze at the sky. Let each child describe the images he sees.

Explore Indoor Environmental Changes

❯ Keep puzzles the same for one week at a time, then change to different puzzles. Mix puzzle pieces from two different puzzles together for a challenge. Work the puzzles without the frames. Work the puzzles upside down without looking at the pictures on the top of each piece.

❯ Vary items in learning centers. Add a box into blocks. Put rubber spatulas to paint with at the easel. Place hats in the block corner or tie streamers on toy cars.

❯ Put manipulatives on a large blanket in the middle of the floor.

❯ Rearrange the classroom furniture and toys for a visual surprise. This should only be done once or

twice over a whole year, as frequent changes of this magnitude can be confusing and disruptive for children.

❯ Change classrooms with another group for one day to explore different toys and room arrangements.

❯ Plan a treasure hunt for the snack. Follow simple maps to the hidden food. Mark the path as you hike. Have children draw maps of the path taken.

❯ Incorporate theme days for fun and variety. Instead of all the usual interest areas, have all areas include items that revolve around one theme. This attracts the children's attention and increases their desire to participate in the activity.

• Baby day: Have children bring in a baby doll. Provide extra dolls for children who don't have one. Build houses for the dolls in the block area. Cook for and take care of the baby dolls in the family living area. Count, weigh, and measure the dolls to determine size; then chart the results. Wash baby dolls in the water table. Set up an area with infant toys. Put books about babies and baby board books in the book area. Listen to baby songs and lullabies. Eat baby food fruit for snack.

• Block day: Use a variety of blocks in the different play areas. Put floor blocks in the block area and small blocks in the family living area that can be used as food in cooking activities. Place snap blocks, Lego blocks, bristle blocks, and colored blocks on tables. Put books that depict building houses or playing with blocks in the library area. Print with plastic blocks dipped in paint. A variation of this for older children is Lego day: use a variety of Lego blocks to build.

• Moving day: Wagons, suitcases, and boxes are added to all areas. Children are encouraged to fold, pack, and move toys and equipment to a new destination in the room. Unpacking and putting away items occupies children as you prepare new signs for the shelves. Later, move everything back to the original storage space unless you decide to leave everything in the new configuration. This is a good activity when a child is moving to a new house or city.

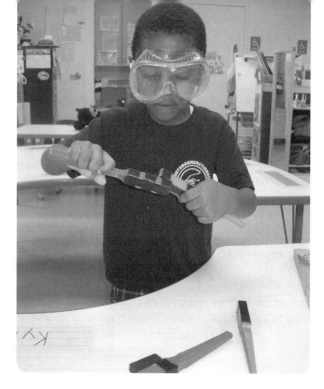

dumping them out has no appeal, but arranging the table to simulate or highlight a theme will attract children and help them focus on the planned outcomes. Again, you are the catalyst who narrates the action taking place, asks questions, and helps the child learn from the experience. There is no limit to the themes, but ideas will pop up as the children's interest is sparked during field trips or everyday experiences. Here are some ideas to try.

PRESCHOOL ACTIVITIES

Use Prop Boxes

❯ Appliance repair: Take apart and "repair" broken appliances, radios, and toys with pliers, screwdrivers, and hammers. This activity requires extra supervision.

❯ Nut box: Put a variety of nuts with nutcrackers, magnifying glasses, and small hammers in the box for children to look at, feel, count, classify, sort, and taste (check for allergies). Add books on different kinds of nuts and storybooks about nuts and squirrels.

❯ Nature box: Have different sizes and shapes of shells with a shell book, leaves and a leaf book, or rocks with a rock book. Add magnifying glasses for classifying and sorting. Include glue, cardboard, and markers for art projects.

• Cleaning day: Let children be involved in washing down furniture with wet sponges and large towels. Smocks and doll clothes can be washed in water tables or buckets and hung on clotheslines (outside is ideal). Riding toys go though the "car wash" outside. Scrub brushes and water clean the paved areas. Wash the chalkboard and walls inside. Scrub easels with large floor scrub brushes to take off the caked paint. This is messy but fun! Great for a summer day!

• Slumber party: Wear pajamas and slippers. Lie on mats to play with table toys. Play lullabies, read *Ira Sleeps Over* by Bernard Waber, *Goodnight Moon* by Margaret Wise Brown, and *Spot Sleeps Over* by Eric Hill. Drink cocoa.

Tabletop Prop Boxes

A prop box has objects around one theme and can be easily stored and then placed on a table to engage one or two children at a time. Prop boxes help keep learning fresh and relevant. Boxes should be well organized and well supplied. Add an experience box or prop box into the environment to spark different exploration and thinking skills. Children can safely explore, experiment, and try out new ideas, augmenting their intellectual development. How you place the objects makes a difference. Just

Group Time

There is no limit to the activities that create an optimum environment for children to think and learn during the routine of the day. Only your imagination will limit the variety of tasks. Make group time active, not passive. Reduce sitting and listening time. Involving more senses increases the placement of information into memory. If only one child can count at a time, then the others either aren't focusing or are only partially attending. Therefore, to get the most out of group time, each child should have objects to count or discuss.

Group time must be well planned. Even the most experienced teacher cannot "wing" a group. Look at the class goals and objectives and select activities that enhance the skills. Make sure you plan more than you have time to do. If you are reading a book you think is interesting but find that none of the children are paying attention, close the book, even if it's not finished, and move on to another planned portion. Be flexible.

Group times should be kept short, with many different activities and transitions to keep children engaged. Some children are not ready to sit in groups even at three or four years of age. When forced to sit, they will become disruptive and distract others. Find a quiet, solitary activity for a child unable to sit through group time. Group time should not be more than fifteen to twenty minutes for three-year-olds and limited to thirty minutes for four-year-olds. Circle time should have transitions that join active and passive topics. When introducing new activities, keep the expectations low and remember the children's age and abilities.

Fine Arts

Today there is pressure to eliminate or decrease time spent in art activities and increase academic tasks. Eliminating fine arts is a mistake. Thinking and problem-solving skills, mathematical patterns, gross-motor and fine-motor skills, plus creativity are outcomes of fine art participation. Children learn to think differently and, in the process, strengthen brain pathways.

Fine art projects are often a release for emotions. Children can learn to express their feelings through art, clay, dance, or music. It is imperative, however, that children have free choice of activities and that not all children are required to do the same thing. When children are forced to "paint a yellow flower" or "draw a whale," they will do it to please the adult rather than as a form of creative expression.

When children participate in creating music, dance, literature, theater arts, and visual arts at an early age, they not only learn about the fine art, they also learn to appreciate culture. Look at various native art reproductions and sculptures. Learn dance steps from different countries. Use cultural stories like *Bringing the Rain to Kapiti Plain* by Verna Aardema for creative dramatics.

Make sure art activities are at children's level. Many young children are not ready for formal lessons and may not have the large and small musculature for success. The lessons may generate anxiety, stress, and fear. This leads to problems that will hamper all learning. Singing age-appropriate songs, having enjoyable musical experiences geared to their age level, and receiving positive reinforcement for experimentation with a variety of rhythms using creative dance or musical instruments are more valuable experiences. The use of fine arts should be integrated with all other areas of the curriculum. Helping children explore varied art media, dance, music, creative movement, and dramatic play within the study of another subject helps to bring sense and meaning to the activity (Copple and Bredekamp 2009).

PRESCHOOL ACTIVITIES

Encourage Art Appreciation at Group Time

❯ Look at reproductions of masterpiece paintings. Talk about the colors and what is depicted. Discuss the actions, sounds, and smells represented in the painting. If the picture has animals, have pieces of fake fur to feel.

❯ Assemble fruit and the objects found in still life pictures for children to feel and smell.

- Allow children to caress a sculpture.

- Have clay or paint available for children to experiment with as they view the art objects.

- Arrange flowers in a vase and fruit in a bowl. Give children tempera or water paints and teach them how to look at the object and then paint their interpretation on paper. Don't expect it to look like anything realistic.

Use Puppets at Group Time

Developing activities around puppets provides children with a unique acting situation. Introduce and model puppet manipulation to prevent hitting and biting with puppets. In the beginning, a puppet theater is not necessary and might even create difficulties. Let the children stand behind the back of a chair or kneel behind a low table. Later you can make simple theaters out of large boxes. Stage props can also be distracting when children are just beginning to use puppets.

- Develop a tape recording that teaches children how to manipulate a puppet to eat, sit, dance, cry, laugh, and sleep. Put the tape in the listening center. Everyone listening to the recording needs a puppet to move. Later place the recording in the dramatic play area to offer more experience with moving puppets.

- Read a story as the children move and control their puppets. *The Poky Little Puppy* by Janette Sebring Lowrey and Gustaf Tenggren, *Chicken Little*, and *Gingerbread Boy* are easy to act out.

- Sing a song or fingerplay as children create a story with puppets. "The Wheels on the Bus," "Old Mac-Donald Had a Farm," and "The Bear Went over the Mountain" are simple puppet plays.

- Sit in a circle. Hold a puppet and talk about classroom problems, such as no one cleaning up the block area. Pass the puppet to each child to propose solutions.

Support Dramatic Play at Group Time

- Teach children how to pretend through mime. Act out popcorn kernels frying in a pan, hungry kittens looking for food, driving a car, or fishing on a sunny day. Imitate a washing machine, lawn mower, or playing tennis.

- Teach children how to act out a task using the game of charades.

- Act out a song that tells a story, such as "Baby Beluga" by Raffi, "The Little Gray Ponies Are Sleeping," "The Little White Duck," or "The Ants Go Marching." Use a tape or let a few children sing as others act out the songs. Write up the sequence of events. Change the animal to see how the story and song change.

- Act out familiar fingerplays or nursery rhymes, such as "Five Little Monkeys Swinging in a Tree," "Five Green and Speckled Frogs," or "Old King Cole."

- Act out a familiar story. Read the story slowly and direct the movement. It is best to use a small group of children as performers. In the beginning, props and costumes are distracting for the children. Hats don't stay on, paper costumes tear, and often bowls are dropped. After they're familiar with the story, add a few props.

- Invite children to repeat the dialogue you read or create their own dialogue. Don't force children to say what the character has said. After several times acting it out, the dialogue will come. Good stories to start with include *The Tale of Peter Rabbit* by Beatrix Potter, *The Three Billy Goats Gruff*, and *The Gingerbread Boy*.

- Act out predicable stories that have verses that repeat. *Caps for Sale* by Esphyr Slobodkina allows all children to participate at the same time, pretending to be the monkeys.

Dance at Group Time

- Simplify Israeli, Russian, Mexican, Greek, and other ethnic dances so that children understand the unique steps. The music and beat differ with each culture. Dance the "Mexican Hat Dance" or the Israeli "Hora."

- Teach square dancing steps. Do-si-do, swing your partner, and promenade are all steps that are easily taught. Slow down the music and directions so children can follow.

- Use records, drum beats, and voice chants as children dance. African rhythms lend themselves easily to young children's abilities and allow them to learn about a rich cultural heritage.

- Invite a local dance studio to bring students to perform. Children can watch and learn to enjoy ballet, tap, and jazz. Watch excerpts of "Swan Lake," "The Nutcracker," or the ballet "Cinderella."

- Sway scarves or ribbons as children move to music of varied tempos, creating their own original dances.

Support Interactive Group Time

- Let each child use a car, truck, train, or boat as you discuss transportation.

- Give everyone five or ten small objects (too large to swallow) to manipulate when counting.

- Make up a group fantasy. Everyone takes turns contributing to the story.

- Read *The Bubble Factory* by Tomie DePaola and create an imaginary world where everyone is made of bubbles. Let children take turns adding adventures about their floating or popping.

- Build an imaginary sandwich. Each child selects an ingredient inside or on top. Illustrate the "mighty munchie mountain sandwich."

- To stretch imaginations, describe experiences of the children in "Upside Down Land," where people walk on their hands and houses rest on their roofs.

- Before opening them, let children guess what is in boxes that arrive at the school. Use the box size and return address to help children strategize.

Learning through Cooking

Children not only love to help prepare food, but in doing so, they engage every sense and activate multiple networks of the brain simultaneously. This is a wonderful opportunity to teach safety, cleanliness, and nutrition. Use food preparation as a time to extend cognitive processes. Create rebus recipe pages to allow young children to read the measurements and ingredients. Mathematics becomes important as ingredients are measured. Science is evident when liquids and solids are mixed and as heat changes the consistency of foods. Discuss how fruits and vegetables grow. Find out how flour and sugar are processed. Write a sequence story about the cooking experience. Children will be eager to sample their own cooking. To create a knowledge base for diversity, cook and taste foods from all cultures. Use a vocabulary that reflects the names of ethnic foods. Also, see pages 22 and 61–63 for more activity suggestions for involving children in cooking.

PRESCHOOL ACTIVITIES

Introduce Foods from around the World

❱ Put out bowls of chopped cucumber, tomato, lettuce, and feta cheese, and let children fill their own pita pockets (Greek).

❱ Eat rice with fingers or chopsticks (Asian).

❱ Try ugali, also known as cornmeal porridge (Kenyan).

❱ Drink hot tea with rice crackers (Japanese) or scones (English).

❱ Fry plantains or bananas (Puerto Rican).

❱ Make a version of a blintz (Russian). Flatten a slice of bread with a rolling pin. Spread with cream cheese and sprinkle with cinnamon sugar. Roll up. Fry lightly in butter until brown.

❱ Compare the taste of pita (Greek/Middle Eastern), matzo (Israeli), and baguette bread (French).

❱ Taste and discuss the differences in rice noodles (Chinese) and pasta (Italian).

ALL CHILDREN LEARN THROUGH PLAY

Play is innate and is an integral part of a young child's life. Play must be a part of any early childhood environment. It helps children adjust to new situations, and it enhances learning readiness. Through play, children practice behavior and problem solving skills. As young children play, they are developing motor and language skills as well as social skills such as sharing and negotiating. Chil-

dren learn better from play activities than from direct instruction. Play is serious and is real learning (Frost et al. 2007).

Play that comes after learning takes place allows the learning to be internalized. Children practice what they know. It allows children to rehearse the information and helps them move the information into permanent memory. Play really allows children to reach their potential.

Don't think that putting just any toys into the environment satisfies the need to play. Many toys are designed as learning devices; they are meant to teach something. Children need free time to explore and create fantasies with open-ended play materials, such as blocks, dolls, dress-up clothes, and hats. They can then use their own skills and imagination to create play scenarios. When children play, they become ready for advanced ways of viewing and thinking about their world. They can learn self-control and improve their literacy skills through mature, dramatic play that encompasses multiple children who create complex dramatic play scenarios (Bodrova 2008).

Create environments that encourage play with diverse materials (Drew and Rankin 2004). A child takes a puzzle piece and, instead of placing it inside the puzzle, zooms it along the table and down the table leg like a car. The child turns a chair into a bus or a doghouse for a stuffed animal. Children's imaginations must be valued. Play can increase vocabulary, provide solutions to problems, help children learn socialization skills, and allow them to master their ever-changing emotions.

Too many toys, too much noise and activity, or too much stimulation are as harmful as a bare environment and limited play. Overstimulation has a negative effect on the brain development of young children. Young children need a balance of play, quiet time, and hands-on activity to thrive.

Interest Centers

Most early child classrooms have defined work areas called learning or interest centers. The most common centers are blocks; dramatic play or family living; sensory, cognitive and manipulative; art;

discovery or science; and library. A large, unencumbered area with definite boundaries is needed for blocks. This area can be combined with or near the transportation area. The dramatic play corner is also nearby so that play can spill over from one area to the next. Children can build roads, put cars on them, and add signs. After building a house, children can don fire hats and use hoses to put out the fire or line up chairs to create a car or bus to add to the experience. The dramatic play area has props from real life, with a child-size kitchen, bedroom, or laundry area, and includes multicultural dolls and dress-up clothes. The sensory, cognitive, and manipulative area is full of puzzles, games, and materials that help children learn on their own. There is a sensory area to sift and pour sand or water, an art area to promote creativity, and a discovery or science area for learning about nature and scientific principles. The library area abounds with books of all sizes about every imaginable theme and representative of diverse cultures and inclusive families. These days, schools have added computers. The areas remain stable, but the contents of the areas vary from time to time.

Children are free to explore within each area. These areas need to be accessible to children most of the day, if possible, but a minimum of an uninterrupted hour in the morning and another hour in the afternoon is a must. Children need to be free to choose where to play and how long to stay in each area. Richly furnished areas foster children's creativity and stimulate their imaginations. All domains and senses are aroused.

Establish a system and a routine so that areas remain neat and organized and only contain the number of children the area can accommodate. Movement through the interest areas can be easily taught to older toddlers and preschool children. Some programs use a ticket system to help regulate the movement to and between interest areas. This limits the number of children who can play simultaneously in the space based on the amount of equipment.

Sitting the children down, explaining where they can go, and asking them to choose an area to begin their play helps them focus on where they want to play. Children can organize their thoughts and learn how to plan their time. The process also allows you to manage the number of children going to each learning area. Children then walk to the area one by one and start the exploration and manipulation of the materials available. This prevents the chaos of children running to be first into a spot.

Some commercially available curricula have a process where children plan what to do, experience the activity, and then review what was done. This process of rehearsal and discussion enhances the learning process and helps move information into working memory (Sousa 2008). Piaget argued that children learn primarily from their own spontaneous exploration of things and a subsequent reflective abstraction from those activities. Memory is strengthened by repetition, intensity, and frequency of practice (Jensen 2005). You can easily implement this strategy.

As children play in interest areas, they are building the following intellectual skills:

- Sequencing involved in planning a project and completing it

- Increasing attention span

- Learning scientific principles, such as gravity, leverage, and balance

- Developing creativity and using imagination

- Exercising choices

- Deciding which direction the pencil or brush will go: deciding when and where on the page

- Practicing decision-making skills

- Deciding on which colors or shapes to use

- Attempting to create by filling a space

- Feeling successful

- Enjoying learning new facts

- Experiencing excitement, joy, or disappointment

- Increasing the ability to focus

- Learning that nature often follows a pattern

- Discovering through trial and error

- Learning to take risks

- Learning to delay gratification until a project is completed

The Importance of Open-Ended Questions

During play, children are allowed to create and direct their play using their own ideas. You can help children problem solve by using open-ended questions, which are questions that cannot be answered with a "yes," "no," or a one-word answer. Open-ended questions encourage conversation. Teach children how to weigh the pros and cons when making decisions by modeling it for them. After a while, they will begin to use the technique (Willis and Schiller 2011). Lead children to think through problems and predict outcomes. You can choose to stand back and observe briefly or extend play with suggestions and directed questions.

It is important that adults do not dominate the play. They can be involved in the tea party or as a household member to model how to play in the family living area and can suggest ways to move the plot forward. However, adults should not direct everything, because then creativity disappears and children lose the benefits of play. Your role is to stimulate thought processes, build vocabulary,

and help the children establish educated guesses. Help guide children in finding resources to answer questions and make suggestions for outcomes. Enhance the value of child-initiated and child-directed play by supporting children, which adds dimension and builds cognition. Move around the interest centers, interacting with the children as they play, and ask open-ended questions to stimulate critical-thinking skills.

PRESCHOOL ACTIVITIES

Ask Open-Ended Questions in the Dramatic Play Area

❯ "What kind of work do you do, Daddy?"

❯ "How are you going to cook the eggs?"

❯ "Why do you think your baby is crying?"

❯ "What would happen if we put your pancakes in the oven?"

❯ "If you put the ice cream in the refrigerator, what will happen?"

❯ "How can we make room for two more children?"

PRESCHOOL ACTIVITIES

Ask Open-Ended Questions in the Block Area

❯ "Tell me about your building."

❯ "How could a person get into your box house?"

❯ "How were you able to make this tower so tall?"

❯ "What would happen if we removed this block?"

❯ "How would the tower change if you added this rectangle on top?"

❯ "What shapes can you make from these two blocks?"

Ask Open-Ended Questions in the Art Area

❯ "Tell me about your drawing."

❯ "How did you make so many shades of green?"

❯ "How did you make those stripes?"

❯ "What colors can you make by combining the colors at your easel?"

❯ "How did you create this unique design?"

❯ "Why do you think your picture is taking such a long time to dry?"

Ask Open-Ended Questions in the Discovery Area

❯ "What do you think caused the plant to die?"

❯ "How do you think the hamster got to the top of the cage?"

❯ "Why did the big wooden block float and the little penny sink?"

❯ "What would happen if we put the plant in the closet?"

❯ "How can we keep the rabbits out of the garden?"

❯ "Why do you think one fish died and the other fish didn't?"

Peer Teaching during Learning Areas

Our brains are the most engaged when we are teaching something we know to someone else. You can create opportunities for one child to transfer knowledge to another. Peer teaching is advantageous for both children. The child who assumes the teacher role is gaining self-esteem. For a child to explain how to put a puzzle together to another child who struggles to assemble the pieces, the child teaching has to have an understanding of the process. She is using her spatial knowledge and reviewing what she knows. Her communication skills will be enhanced as she explains the puzzle assembly. The child who is unable to work the puzzle will get one-to-one attention from a peer. Often the teaching child has a different approach that will help the struggling child understand how to manipulate the pieces.

PRESCHOOL ACTIVITIES

Support Peer Teaching in Learning Areas

> Children who easily put together puzzles work with others who struggle.

> One child helps another complete parquetry or block patterns.

> One child describes pictures to other children as they "read" a book.

> One child explains to another child how to build a tower or how to mix colors.

> A child retells a favorite story to another child. Switch roles so both children tell a story.

Dramatic Play or Family Living Area

Imaginative play situations in the dramatic play area require very complicated thought processes and are very enriching—many parts of the brain are engaged. The thinking necessary to create a play scenario is at a much higher level than activities such as working puzzles or arranging dominoes. Many people think playing dress-up and cooking pretend food is not learning time. Conversely, children acquire more knowledge in a shorter span of time than in some so-called learning activities. Children must think, problem solve, interact with others, and manipulate objects in a short span of time, creating a rich environment for brain growth. Emotions play a large role in this area because children recreate feelings as well as situations. Pre-reading skills are practiced because the activities reinforce language and help add new vocabulary. Complex scenarios require cognitive and problem-solving skills. The complexity of the play varies by the richness of the area. Try to ensure that there are enough supplies to support the play and the number of children the area allows (Phelps 2003).

Dramatic Play Area Supplies

Equip the area with a variety of toys to create a homelike atmosphere. Arrangement is crucial. Props cannot be just thrown in a box. When the area is neatly arranged, children can plan and execute their play. Dress-up clothing, hats, and purses or briefcases need to be hung up for children to choose. Dolls need to be in beds, cradles, or high chairs. Dishes and utensils need to be near the stove. A table and chairs need to be in the area so children can prepare, sit, and eat. Once the area is organized, children will take over and play will begin. Having too many items cramped into a small area limits play. Decide which equipment would best fit into the area and spark the interests of the children. Rotate items in and out to prevent having too many articles out at one time and to provide a new and exciting atmosphere. The following list includes ideas for incorporating items that are usually found in a dramatic play area:

- Provide child-size furniture, such as a table and chairs, a toy refrigerator, a stove and sink, a washing machine, an iron and ironing board, and a cabinet to hold supplies.

- Include child-size dishes, tableware, tablecloths, baskets, pots, and pans.

- Have dolls of varying sizes, shades of skin color, and ethnic backgrounds, doll beds, strollers, doll clothes, and baby blankets.

- Provide male and female dress-up clothes that are easy for children to put on and take off. Instead of having adult clothes, go to thrift stores and buy children's sport coats, ties, fancy dresses, and vests.

- Supply several purses, wallets, and brief cases as well as an assortment of hats and scarves.

- Include a variety of shoes: tap and ballet shoes, boots, and slippers.

- Bring in real or silk flowers of all colors.

- Display colorful posters of diverse family groups, career workers, and people doing household chores.

- Add brooms, mops, and other pretend cleaning supplies. Provide empty boxes and bottles of nontoxic cleaning products.

- Have toy fruits, vegetables, and replicas of prepared foods. Use generic objects for children to pretend with.

- Put out toy or old telephones along with boxes of index cards with the children's names and phone numbers.

- Keep a supply of paper, pencils, and clipboards.

Dramatic Play Area Prop Boxes

To change the scope of the play, add boxes of supplies to the dramatic play area on an occasional basis. The box can contain items around a theme to make setup, cleanup, and storage easy. Open a box and arrange the area to resemble the theme before opening the corner to children. Setup is the key to success. Leaving the articles in the box will not promote creative play. Children tend to just dump out the box, sort out the items they want, and begin play. Setting the area to resemble the theme encourages excitement and motivation and helps organize the play:

- Bakery: Add aprons, chef hats, flour shakers, sifters, plastic bowls, wooden spoons, oven mitts, rolling pins, cookie cutters, cake pans, and muffin tins to the kitchen area. Playdough and flour can be added.

- Office: Put out typewriters, telephones, adding machines with tape, expired checkbooks, ink pads with rubber stamps, envelopes, stickers, a variety of scratch paper, and a multitude of pens and pencils. Briefcases and cardboard mailboxes add to the experience.

- Medical office: Provide paper surgical gowns (cut to child length), face masks, hats, latex gloves, stethoscopes, blood pressure cuffs, wrap bandages, and tongue depressors (all donated by physicians or a hospital). Toy doctor kits, gauze bandages, tape, and adhesive bandages add to the area. To help complete the play experience, have mats for the patients to lie down on.

- Barber or beauty shop: Put out craft sticks for pretend shaving. Provide a mirror for the children to watch themselves. You can include a full-length mirror by placing it face up on a table, or you can provide individual makeup mirrors. Have brushes, curlers, and curling irons with the cords removed to use with wigs on head stands, and bowls of soapy water with fingernail brushes in the beauty area. New (to the children) jewelry, scarves, and hats change the play. Add chairs and magazines and show children how to place medium-size paper bags over their hair to simulate hair dryers. Encourage boys and girls to try all activities.

- Grocery store: Arrange empty boxes from healthy foods, empty cans with the rims sanded smooth, used plastic drink and milk cartons, and toy foods on shelves to resemble a store. Cash registers, toy money (just pretending is fine, also), aprons for the clerks, old credit cards or plastic hotel keys, and grocery paper and plastic bags add to the reality. Toy carts or baby buggies allow customers to buy and take the items "home."

- Pet shop, shoe store, restaurant, post office, and shoe repair: Assemble items or prop boxes for making other interesting experiences. Use the children's interests and personal experiences to guide you to create more boxes. Keep the boxes well labeled with lists of enclosed items. Be sure to replenish supplies as they are consumed so the box is ready the next time it is brought out for play.

Art Area

The art area is appealing to many children because of its inherent messiness, its variety of activities, and its relaxed atmosphere. A good art area allows a child to be independent and experience a diversity of action. The activities allow for choice and are open-ended so each project is truly the child's creation. Art helps the child develop cognitive, physical, emotional, and social skills. Children can express feelings concretely and can also feel a sense of accomplishment when they see their creations. Children can dabble in the art area daily and never get tired of it. Learning is taking place each time the child approaches the same activity. In the beginning, art is purely kinesthetic. After children begin

to master the physical ability of using a brush, glue, marker, or scissors, they move on to master color, arrangement, and patterns. Each time they repeat an activity, they are establishing pathways in many parts of the brain and working toward mastering that task. They use the knowledge gained in the previous attempts, propelling themselves into the next level, creating new connections. Soon children can think about their creations without having to direct the muscles of their hands, fingers, and arms to move when they draw or paint. Only if these connections are reinforced through repetition will they approach permanence.

Preschool children new to art will go through the same developmental stages of art that an older infant and toddler goes through, only faster. The first stage is a disordered scribble. Children enjoy feeling their muscles move as they try to make a mark on the paper. This random coloring then modifies into purposeful movements as the child begins to control the crayon or paintbrush. The child picks up paintbrushes, changes colors, and even attempts to join lines. He is beginning to make shapes (whether accidental or purposeful) and may name his scribbles. Often children in preschool and kindergarten do not leave this stage. Others move on to draw representational objects that adults can recognize, such as faces, people, and houses.

Children need practice cutting with child-size scissors. Anything they cannot cut out by themselves is too difficult for their developmental level. Be cautious about using teacher-provided projects such as precut patterns to glue or ditto-sheet objects to color or cut. Adults coordinate their eyes and hands as they cut on the lines. They use thought processes to put pieces together to form a recognizable picture. Adults learn at a rapid rate, reinforcing and refining skills, and problem solving. Children are not learning these things. Likewise, when directed, children can assemble forms without having to use any thinking processes, only fine-motor skills. Teacher-directed crafts are a lesson in following directions, not art. Teacher-directed crafts not only fail to promote comprehension and skill formation, they also douse creativity. Remember, it is the process of creating the art, not the end

product, that has value. Art activities should be open-ended and entirely based on the ideas of the child. Put out supplies and let the child decide how to use them. No two end products look alike. When a child chooses art supplies and creates a drawing (even if it is scribbles) and cuts the paper independently (even if it ends up as scraps), then the child is thinking and making decisions.

As children repeat—or practice—activities in rich environments, brain communication for those activities becomes more efficient, faster. With practice, the speed with which a child can complete an action increases, which is evidence of these stronger and more efficient brain networks. Not only must the child conceptualize what she wants to create using different media, but she must also use gross- and fine-motor skills and hand-eye coordination to execute color, patterns, and shapes. Multiple parts of the brain are involved in coordinating thought. When children practice using brushes, crayons, and markers, they strengthen the efficiency of the networks in their brains. Creativity is a higher level of brain function.

Supplies on the Art Shelves

Art supplies should be at eye level and accessible to children without an adult doling them out. Cover tables with a protective material, such as newspaper, so children can create without worrying about going off their own sheets of paper. Give children choices from a wide variety of art activities using one differing medium every day. It is important to give children experiences using different types of art supplies, as it is the process, not the end product, that has the value. Do not overwhelm children with a large variety of choices. Some supplies are always available, such as an easel, paper, painting implements, and a sculpture medium. Each day add one new experience.

Children should be allowed to stay in the art area and repeat activities (several collages or three easel paintings) as long as their interest dictates. Your creativity can enhance the type of supplies available at any given time. The following are some ways to equip an art area for an early childhood setting:

- Provide smocks.

- Put large and small pencils, multicolored crayons, and washable markers in containers so that children can select the colors and sizes that suit their needs.

- Include stamps, ink pads, and dot-art markers.

- Add fingerpaint or colored glue.

- Keep a variety of paper available, including colored construction paper in several sizes, newsprint, old computer and office paper, and wallpaper books. Have a variety of cardboard, paper plates, container lids, and foam trays.

- Include bubble wrap, corrugated cardboard, and netting to inspire different projects.

- Have washable liquid glue, craft glue, and glue sticks. Provide small glue bottles to squeeze.

- Supply playdough and clay along with rolling pins, cookie cutters, craft sticks, and blunt scissors for cutting.

- Bring in items such as cardboard boxes, paper towel tubes, large material scraps, recyclable items, ribbon, wrapping paper, old greeting cards, and leaves to spark creativity.

- Supply used advertising envelopes so children can put paper scraps inside to take home.

- Keep scissors, masking or Scotch tape, and staplers accessible.

- Provide divided trays filled with collage items, such as a variety of buttons, pom-poms, cotton balls, small material scraps, yarn, colored cellophane, and tissue paper.

Supplies and Activities at the Easel

What better way to learn about colors than through the use of paint? Children use both the large muscles in their arms and the small muscles in their hands while painting. They learn to control their movements as they dip the brush into the paint and apply it to the paper. They need hand-eye coordination to move the paint around and create what they imagine. The brain develops many connections that eventually allow these movements to occur without thought or effort. Once a child has mastered painting at an easel, he can transfer the knowledge to use in other mediums, such as drawing with a marker or making a design while fingerpainting. These are the same motor skills the child will use when writing, only on a larger scale. The more practice and coordination children develop, the easier it is to make the smaller marks necessary for writing letters. Children are thinking and problem solving with every stroke of the brush. In addition, they are using their creativity and imagination.

At holiday times, use colored paper to match the theme: orange paper with black paint around Halloween or red and pink paper for Valentine's Day. Refrain from precutting pumpkins or hearts for the children to use. Remember, this is the child's artwork, not yours. Precut items convey a silent message that the adult's drawing or cutting is the way the finished work should appear. If the child wants hearts or pumpkins, her attempts to create them requires problem solving and hand-eye coordination. The exercise has value for the child and, therefore, the creation is more meaningful. If the child cannot draw or cut the desired shape, then instead you can observe, "You colored a red area for Valentine's Day" or "I can see you painted orange to represent a pumpkin" to validate her work. The following are fun ways to set up the easel so it's inviting for children:

- Set up an easel with twenty-four-inch by thirty-inch newsprint and several colors of paint in nondrip paint cups. Vary paint colors often.

- Supply several sizes of paintbrushes to accommodate each child's preference. Occasionally add different items—such as a scrub brush, a vegetable brush, a wad of newspaper, used gift cards, or a baby bottle brush—to paint with.

- Put yellow paint in one cup and blue in another. Let the children explore to discover green. Repeat with red and blue to make purple and red and yellow to make orange. Add white or black so children can lighten and darken their new colors.

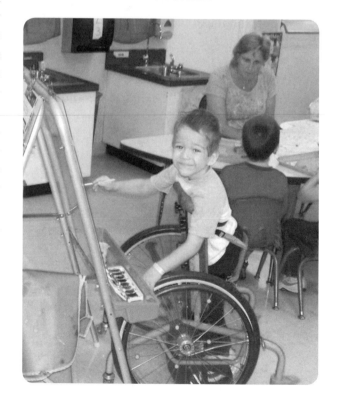

- Place several colors at the easel. You won't have to teach the children to combine colors! Discuss the results.

- Place three drops of different colored paint next to each other using an eyedropper or spoon. Use an old plastic gift card to spread the paint. The colors will blend.

- Provide colored paper instead of newsprint. White paint on black paper encourages a new way of thinking about painting.

Water and Sand Area

Playing in the sand and water tables helps to calm upset children. Here children work side by side, collaborating on digging and pouring. Think of the vast amount of information children will learn while in this area. As they pour and sift, they are learning about gravity. Mathematical concepts are honed as they use measuring cups and related vocabulary of whole and half. Counting the number of cups it takes to fill a pail reinforces one-to-one correspondence. They learn how to think and observe as they experiment with liquids and solids and reach conclusions. Concepts such as sink and float, part and whole, and object permanence are inherent in this area.

Sand and water aren't the only two sensory materials to put into this area. Once again, your imagination and creativity can keep this area ever changing and exciting. For example, make homemade putty by pouring liquid starch over a small amount of white liquid glue. Knead it until it turns to putty. You can add colors to the glue before mixing. Pull it and it breaks. Press it against pencil drawings or some types of newsprint and the putty will pull the picture onto its surface. Any liquid or dry material that is safe for young children can be used. Another fun experience is combining a small amount of water with cornstarch. This mixture is a solid that melts when picked up and becomes a liquid. When left out for a few days, the water evaporates and it turns back into a powdery substance. This provides a new sensory experience and adds scientific information about how solids

and liquids can change. Help children use words to describe the feel of the materials in the different stages. Relate it to the feel of other materials: "This feels smooth and silky like the satin material on the doll's dress." "The dry cornstarch feels exactly like baby powder." Extend what children know by adding facts or by relating one experience to past knowledge. This helps children move information from permanent memory to working memory to combine with new information.

Water tables and sand tables can be in either the art area or the discovery area, or they can stand alone. Use large dishpans or other containers and place them near water for easy cleanup. Check with your licensing agent regarding regulations related to the use and sanitizing of water tables. It is a good practice to have the children wash their hands before entering into water play. The water should be changed after each group of children leaves the table. Washing hands afterward stops the spread of germs.

Supplies in the Water and Sand Area

Change both the items for children to manipulate and the media they play in often to keep children's thinking at a high level. Equip the water and sand tables with pouring and measuring cups, scales, spoons, funnels, and sponges. Children love to play in water, pouring it from one vessel into another.

They like to fill buckets with sand and dump them out. Instead of always using water or sand, think of other safe media you can use, such as potting soil, shredded paper, or new mulch. Not all items should be put out at the same time. Group items that surround a theme. Being intentional in selecting the supplies to help children explore and learn a concept will make the sensory area a valuable activity. Here are examples of both media and supplies to rotate in and out of the area:

- Include multisized cups, pitchers, and bowls, small buckets, small shovels, and containers of every size and shape.

- Have scoops, turkey basters, funnels, measuring cups and spoons, whisks, flour sifters or empty cans with different sized holes, and hand mixers available.

- Supply a variety of natural and synthetic sponges.

- Add mild liquid soap, extracts, or food coloring to water.

- Add confetti or plastic sequins to both water and sand.

- Introduce action sand toys, dump trucks, or toy boats in a variety of sizes and shapes.

- Include a variety of toy water or sand animals.

- Place large rocks in the current medium.

- "Plant" plastic plants and flowers in sand or in clean potting soil.

- Provide shells and small pebbles.

- Add foam packing peanuts.

- Freeze or form mounds of ice using ice cubes made with colored water.

The Discovery or Science Area

The discovery area helps children make hypotheses about their environment and understand changes in nature. All the senses are stimulated and the brain is bombarded with images, sounds, smells, textures, and even tastes. The complexity of the operations allows all parts of the brain to work simultaneously. Thought processes are strengthened as children problem solve or generate and test hypotheses. The thrill of discovery elicits feelings of self-esteem and self-worth. Here are some of the things preschoolers experience when they engage in the discovery area:

- Watching living organisms grow

- Learning the sequential steps in a scientific experiment

- Trying observational techniques

- Observing scientific principles, such as gravity, heat, and growth

- Understanding that plants need water and sunshine

- Knowing the source of sunlight and shade, of light and dark

- Studying outer space and learning what sustains life on earth

Supplies in the Discovery Area

Any place can be used as a discovery area: a windowsill, small tables, or a corner of a room. Inside and out, children are always learning about the world. Cooking, planting a garden, caring for animals, and observing changes in nature create exciting discovery moments. Simple science activities that children can conduct by themselves might inspire future scientific exploration. There is no limit to what can be featured in the discovery area. Look around inside and out!

You can have a theme around one scientific fact or natural item. Having too many things at one time dilutes the impact. Bringing in a variety of leaves to look at under a magnifying glass combined with books and puzzles about leaves helps children classify the learning. They can see and touch a variety of leaves and learn that even though the leaves are all different shapes with different names, they are all living organisms that come from plants. The best way to choose the focus of the area is by being

- Posters and photographs showing natural environments

- Fresh fruits and vegetables to see, feel, smell, and taste

- Books on the featured topic

- A computer to conduct research on the Internet

- Pots or cups, potting soil, seeds, and bulbs

- Materials to conduct simple scientific experiments—such as inflating a balloon by mixing vinegar and baking soda to create gas or observing water change from liquid to a solid (freezing) and back to a liquid (melting)—and pictures of the steps so children can replicate the experiment with minimal help

- A bug box to bring caterpillars, tadpoles, frogs, slugs, worms, and bugs into the room for observation, with instructions for children to release them after a short time

- A variety of leaves, rocks, shells, seeds, and sticks to sort and classify, as well as nuts and nests to display

- Magnets and a variety of metal, plastic, or wood objects

- A scale and yardsticks to weigh and measure children, and small scales and rulers to weigh and measure objects

- Chart paper, pencils, markers, stickers, or crayons for recording observations

- Shelves for collections, such as for multiple shells: a turtle shell, a nutshell, and a seashell

- A vegetable, flower, or butterfly garden and a family member willing to help if you do not garden (It is amazing how with their expertise and advice the gardens succeed.)

alert to your surroundings and cognizant of the children's interests. Gathering pinecones or acorns and exploring their attributes is best in the fall, whereas shell exploration is most relevant when a child returns from a trip to the beach. Don't forget to display the things you are most interested in, such as butterflies, crystals, or rocks. Science experiments can be conducted either by a group or individually, depending upon the activity. Here are some ideas to get you started:

- Nontoxic plants of all sizes throughout the room

- A fish tank or small cage with mice, hamsters, gerbils, hermit crabs, or other small animals and books about the care of the specific fish or animal

- Flowers, sticks, and leaves

- Magnifying lenses and microscopes

Support Learning in the Discovery Area

❯ Put plants, fish, or small pets into the environment for the children to care for daily. Augment this activity with books and photographs.

❯ Place interesting insects and plants under a magnifying lens.

❯ Help children tend plants, inside or outside.

❯ Match leaves from different plants. Use leaves, sticks, and flower petals for nature collages. Encourage children to bring in specimens.

❯ Exhibit a daily "natural wonder" to explore.

❯ Take a variety of walks with different themes. Focus on one element as you take a plant walk, an insect walk, a listening walk, or a color walk. Record children's observations and post the results.

❯ Create an observation area for celery stalks, sweet potatoes, broccoli, radishes, onions, and cauliflower placed in water to sprout roots. Add food coloring to the water.

❯ Plant seeds in cups or on wet sponges. Watch the roots grow. Put some in sunlight and others in a dark closet. Chart the difference.

❯ Collect pinecones, sticks, rocks, or acorns. Line them up by attributes, such as size, shape, or color.

Investigate Science Topics

❯ Clean pennies: Cover the bottom of a shallow pan with vinegar. Provide a bowl of salt. Children can dip pennies in vinegar one at a time and rub them with salt. When they are finished, wash the shiny pennies well in soapy water.

❯ Blow up a balloon: Give each child a small plastic bottle, a balloon, a teaspoon, a child-size pitcher, vinegar, and a box of baking soda. Have the child pour a small amount of vinegar into the bottle. Then place a spoonful of baking soda in the balloon as an adult or another child stretches open the top of the balloon. Place the balloon neck over the bottleneck. Pull up on the balloon so the baking soda falls into the bottle. The gas escaping from the fizzing mixture will inflate the balloon. Be careful removing the balloon from the bottle.

❯ Create a volcano: Children can decorate paper cones and then cut a hole at the end of each cone. For a class project, make a large volcano out of papier-mâché. For either paper cones or a papier-mâché volcano, place a cup directly under the opening. The cup should reach the apex of the cone. Pour in vinegar and add baking soda. The frothy foam will rise and run down the volcano.

❯ Explore different states of water: Children can mix food coloring into water. Have children pour the water into an ice-cube tray using child-size pitchers. Place a craft stick in each and freeze. Use the cubes as paint: as the cubes melt, color will transfer to the paper. Observe water changing from liquid to solid and back to liquid.

❯ Plant a butterfly garden: Establish a garden with plants that are known for drawing butterflies. Children can help water and weed. The flowers draw butterflies, which lay eggs. Once the larva hatch, the children can observe them eating the leaves. The caterpillars turn into chrysalises and eventually metamorphose into butterflies. Supply books about butterflies and caterpillars. Compare butterflies to moths and a cocoon with a chrysalis.

❯ Measure rainfall: Place a receptacle on the fence. Check it after a storm and chart the results. Compare results from one month to the next.

❯ Make predictions: Plant a flower bulb. Children can predict the height and color the flower will be. As it grows, graph the development. Ask the children to predict the color of the flowers in the garden. See how many children guess the correct color. Keep charts of their predictions and compare them to the end result. As another idea, purchase bubble solution and make your own using dishwashing liquid. Let the children predict which will make bigger bubbles. Give the children wands to discern the results.

> Hypothesize and research: Children can develop plans to capture a missing hamster, and you can try their solutions. Ask children what local wild birds eat, and record their ideas. Hang bird feeders with different foods (birdseed, bread, sunflower seeds, nuts). Check daily to see what the birds really ate. Alternately, help children theorize about what ate holes in the leaves in the garden. Make a list (worm, insect, rabbit, bird), and research what actually eats that type of plant.

> Discuss solutions: Use daily problems, such as dividing five cookies among seven children, fixing a broken toy, or having a planned walk interrupted by a rainstorm.

Block Area

If they played with blocks as toddlers, children learned how to manipulate and build with them. They put together a few blocks, stacked them, or laid them out in a line. They began the rudimentary understanding of math as they assembled simple towers and streets. Preschoolers build on that experience and knowledge and expand the scope of it by creating scenarios surrounding a block structure. They expand their mathematical understanding as they combine shapes, compare quantities, and create patterns. They apply principles such as symmetry as they build towers beside their buildings. Children practice math concepts, scientific theories, and language skills in the block area as they use their creativity and imaginations. Thinking is at a high level.

The block area has lots of appeal, in large part because blocks are an open-ended toy. There is no right or wrong way to build with them. Children can be in control of the manipulation and move them around to create many different types of structures. Children can play day after day, year

after year in the block area and never tire of the activity. Repetition of both gross- and fine-motor movements brings about permanence in the brain connections. Thinking is at a high level and creates new pathways. As the child's activity changes from one aspect of play to another, different regions of the brain are being activated. The more time spent building, the more complicated the constructions become. Each creation differs and creates new problems for the child to solve.

Through trial and error, the child learns that the blocks must have a foundation in order to stand. As the child continues to build higher, gravity is a foe. The base must be broadened in order to build higher. No adult can convey this scientific principle. The child must have the hands-on experience of building the tower and watching it fall and then rebuilding the tower. Each time, brain connections are reinforced. It might be accidental the first time the child builds the foundation wider than the top and finally achieves success. The child will need to repeatedly build the structure until she understands how to balance the weight of the blocks to

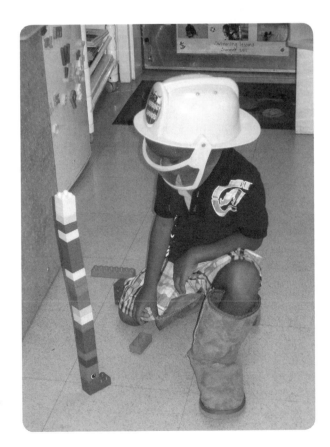

gain height. You can narrate and describe what is happening using task-centered talking. The experience of the blocks, together with the description of the event, leads to cognition.

Teachers often complain that some boys only want to play in the block area and they aren't learning from the other interest areas in the room. It is important to remember that each time the children build, they are expanding their knowledge. If they won't rotate to other areas of the room—and can't be enticed into other areas—add activities to the block area. Extend the learning by bringing in books or asking the children to draw their creations to hang on the wall or write a note saying, "Please leave this block house up." Figure out what you want the child who loves blocks to learn, and create a way to add it to this area. Does he need to learn patterning? Add red, green, blue, and yellow blocks, and challenge the child to build a tower showing a pattern. Once again, your knowledge can guide the play in a different direction so the child gets a well-rounded play experience.

Supplies in the Block Area

As with any area of the classroom, the arrangement and organization of the block area dictates the type of play and building that happens. The number of blocks or the square footage of the block area determines the number of children who can play in the area. Best practices suggest that up to five children should have 150 to 200 unit blocks to build with (Chalufour and Worth 2004). If more than five children play in the block area, include even more blocks. Fewer blocks limit construction, and children cannot expand their thinking to encompass all that could be learned. If you don't have that many blocks, be sure to add other items that can be used in conjunction with the blocks, such as ramps, boxes, or a bench. When blocks are thrown in a box or on a shelf, they are not very appealing. Having a container encourages children to dump out the blocks and dig through a pile to find the ones they want. Most early childhood programs have shelves where blocks are sorted by size and shape. Often a picture of each block is attached to the back of the shelf, helping children to categorize by shape and size as well as put them away neatly. The area is arranged so that children can find the blocks needed for their construction.

Children feel comfortable and secure when the block area is predictable: the blocks remain in one spot, cars and trucks or other additions have a designated place. Within those spaces, rotate items in and out, leaving the objects that add to the block play for a week or more. This allows for lots of experimentation and expansion of ideas. Make sure to change the additions from time to time. If you don't, children won't experience the excitement of something new. As in all areas of the classroom, use task-centered talking as well as open-ended questions to extend the learning. In addition to unit blocks, the following are basic components of a well-equipped block area:

- Toy people and animals

- Large and small cars, a variety of trucks, and toy street signs

- A train set

- Hard hats

- Toy buildings

- Paper, masking tape, and markers or crayons for signs

- Other block sets for variety:
  - Small colored blocks
  - Huge cardboard blocks
  - Lego and snap blocks
  - Popular block sets on the market

PRESCHOOL ACTIVITIES

Support Learning in the Block Area

➤ Construction site: Create a building site with hard hats, pretend tools, aprons, large dump trucks, tow trucks, and cranes.

❯ Painters: Provide paper painter hats, new large wall brushes and paint rollers, empty buckets or paint cans, and painter's aprons.

❯ Simple machines: (Ask for help from a hardware store.)

- Supply large, flat lightweight boards or strips of wall molding with blocks to make inclined planes. Roll small cars, balls, or large marbles down the incline. (Do not use with very young children.) Find out if the size of the rolling object affects the speed. What happens when the angle of the board is changed? Does that make the car or ball increase or decrease speed?

- Create a fulcrum from blocks and a flat board. Balance the board by putting toys on each end.

- Add a pulley and rope to move blocks in small buckets.

Manipulative Play

The manipulative area is an important cognitive area of the classroom. Here children can select from a variety of toys that are gauged to increase their knowledge by reinforcing math, language, and scientific concepts. Manipulatives also help children refine fine-motor skills and encourage critical-thinking and problem-solving skills. Working with a variety of games and toys, children reinforce their language and math skills.

Make sure the shelves are neat and that manipulatives are organized and contained, often in tubs or boxes. Children should be able to spot the manipulative activity that appeals to them without having to sort through lots of boxes or ask for assistance. Containers also help keep the many pieces of an activity from getting lost. Rotate half of the supplies every few weeks so that children who are learning with an item can have sufficient time to experiment, but those who have mastered it can move on to another activity that is more challenging. Items in this area fit nicely in front of a child seated at a table or on a rug square on the floor. Some items are suited for individual manipulation, and others are geared for small groups. Once again,

you are the catalyst to learning, and you can expand the self-exploration with intentional teaching.

Supplies in the Manipulative Area

Many manipulative options are available through supply catalogs, or you can create your own. The list is endless. The manipulative area should include open-ended supplies that can be used in a variety of ways. This area can also include structured, or "closed," activities that only have one "right" way of being solved, such as puzzles. Children should be given the opportunity to use all of the materials creatively as well as to reinforce or learn specific skills. The following are some manipulatives common in preschool classrooms:

- A variety of sizes and shapes of beads along with strings, and patterns to follow

- Pegboards and pegs with rubber bands for creating shapes and pattern cards to follow

- A large variety of letter and number activities, such as magnetic letters and numbers with a magnetic board, matching games, and playing cards

- Parquetry shapes and colored blocks with pattern and mathematical cards

- A variety of puzzles from simple to complex to meet individual needs

- A variety of items for sorting, matching, and classifying or purchased sorting, matching, and classifying games

- Board games, such as "Candy Land" or "Chutes and Ladders"

- Bingo and lotto games

- Dominoes

- Lacing cards

- Small building sets, including magnetic shapes, bristle blocks, and Lego blocks

- Stackable and nesting shapes

- Large cardboard clocks with movable hands

Intellectual Development of Mathematics

Young children are developing an understanding of whole numbers, including counting and quantity. They are learning to identify shapes and repeat patterns. Use numbers, number concepts, and math vocabulary throughout the day. Just as you create a print-rich environment, create a numeral-rich environment as well (NAEYC and NCTM 2010).

Three-year-old children understand that numbers represent quantities and have begun adding numbers into their descriptions: "I want two cookies." Counting and knowing one-to-one correspondence is more complex. Often young children can rote count to ten or twenty but have no idea what constitutes the quantity. It takes lots of experience counting pennies, grapes, and cereal rounds to understand that the word "five" represents five items. Until a child understands that the last number counted represents the total number of items in a group, she will not be able to add or subtract. Once a child learns the concept, he can answer the question "If I gave you one more, how many would you have?" without going back and starting to recount the original quantity (Sousa 2008). A child who has experience counting a variety of items in different ways learns this concept.

Children often use math during their daily activities. They sort, classify, and compare quantities. They notice shapes and patterns as they interact with materials. You can point out the mathematical theory and extend mathematical understanding. Ask the child, "Which pile has more?" "How many do you have all together?" "How many would you have if I gave you one more?" or "That triangle is a different shape than the block over there. What is the difference?"

Adding numerals to quantities helps children understand that the number symbol represents a group of objects. A child needs to have experiences that tie the printed number to the quantity. If they are to have any meaning, number symbols cannot be taught in isolation. Eventually, after multiple experiences manipulating six dolls in play or six pom-poms on an art project, along with seeing the numeral 6, the child will understand that "6" represents the quantity of six items.

Children need to learn how to quantify groups of objects without counting. Most adults can identify quantities up to seven just by seeing a pattern of objects. Playing with dominoes and playing cards lets children practice seeing dots or hearts in a set pattern. Create opportunities for children to see different patterns of quantities between two and ten. String beads, follow block patterns, and use parquetry shapes to practice seeing patterns in a variety of formations.

Children can learn higher-level mathematical thinking at an early age. Dividing apples into quarters and pies into six slices to give each person a piece provides concrete example of division. Cooking is the perfect opportunity to show quantity and to link the numbers in a recipe to the action. Math can become an integral part of everyday play. Children can practice many mathematical skills while playing in interest areas:

- Increasing mathematical vocabulary

- Understanding numerals

- Identifying shapes

- Exploring quantity and using mathematical terms, including more, less, bigger, smaller, taller, shorter, and equal

- Experimenting with length, measurement, and weight

- Understanding wholes and parts

- Practicing matching

- Classifying objects

- Repeating patterns

- Learning about money

- Using sequencing

- Using time concepts, such as morning, tomorrow, later, and after

Introduce Mathematical Concepts

❯ Count objects and talk about how many more are needed for an activity or to reach a higher number.

❯ Count spaces on board games to move the marker and predict how many more spaces are needed to win. Play games that show quantities in patterns, such as card games, board games, and dominoes.

❯ Count calendar squares to discover the number of days until a special event. Record the number of children who came to school each day in the week. Compare the number of days in each month.

❯ Build with unit blocks of various shapes and sizes. Compare the height and width of block buildings and towers by estimating and counting blocks. Predict which block shape is needed to complete the structure.

❯ Manipulate parquetry and attribute blocks to see variations in shape, size, color, and thickness. Sort and classify them or repeat the same formation several times.

❯ String beads, use pegboards, and manipulate colored blocks to create patterns. Repeat patterns—red, blue, green; red, blue, green—then replicate the pattern using a different medium, such as with paint, by gluing sequins or colored paper squares, or arranging balls of colored playdough.

❯ Put rubber bands on pegs in pegboards to create different shapes. Count the number of triangles, rectangles, and squares. Count the number of corners and straight sides in each. Count the total number of corners or straight sizes. Compare the quantities.

❯ Read counting books. Take the time to let the child count the number of objects in the picture on each page. Compare the number of objects on one page and on a different page using quantitative vocabulary. For example, *Then the Doorbell Rang* by Pat Hutchins describes children counting cookies to share.

❯ Identify ways to divide the children into two groups—such as by color of clothing or type of shoes—and then put the two groups together to demonstrate addition. The two numbers will vary, but the total will always be the same!

❯ Use positional words when children are in a line to identify who is first, in the middle, and last. When serving food, use math vocabulary, such as "first" and "next," in addition to numbers. Point out that Jimmy is sitting between Zachary and Olivia or the red square is between the blue triangle and the green rectangle in the pattern.

❯ Use ordinal numbers, such as "first," "second," or "third," to describe the sequence of an activity.

❯ Change the words in Ella Jenkins's chant "Stop and Go" to count the children using a variety of number concepts: first, second, third, and fourth, or one, two, three, and four.

❯ Recite nursery rhymes and fingerplays with number concepts. Recite many counting rhymes in singsong. How many sheep are in "Little Bo Peep" or fiddlers in "Old King Cole"? Look at different books with the same rhymes. It is likely that the pictures will have a different number of people or animals.

❯ Count by twos, fives, and tens. Count backwards.

❯ Sort objects by color, shape, and size. Count the number of each. Use positional and ordinal vocabulary. Relate the counting to numerals. Make graphs and charts comparing the results.

❯ Plant seeds. Have the children predict how many will sprout. Create a graph of the predictions. After the plants have begun to grow, go back and, with a different color marker, graph the actual results. Compare the two quantities.

❯ Graph the color of shoes, size of stuffed animals, height of children, length of strung beads, or number of books on the library shelf. Seeing a comparison of numbers is helpful in learning numerical concepts.

- Count blocks in a tower, pennies collected for a donation, or the number of squares in a picture.

- Design simple problem-solving challenges: "How many different ways can you use to get this object across the room?" List the ways, and then count them. Record the total number.

- Guess how many objects are in a bag just by feeling them. Open the bag and check the answer.

- Teach children how to estimate. Fill different size jars with marbles. Ask the children to guess the quantities. Chart their answers. Count as a group.

- Figure out how to reduce the number of paper towels being used per day to eliminate waste. Count before and after using rubber gloves. Include discussion of recycling and cutting down waste.

- Count piles of pennies, nickels, and dimes. Play with money in the dramatic play area. Decide what could be bought with a specific amount of money.

- Measure tables, chair height, size of block structures, and other items in the room with lengths of yarn, craft sticks, or hand span first. After the children understand the process, measure with rulers, yard sticks, or measuring tapes. Write the length on charts for comparison. Use measurement terms, such as "longer," "shorter," and "equal," and add vocabulary words, such as "inch," "foot," and "yard."

- Use buckets to weigh different types of blocks and graph the results. Use scales that have dual buckets to try to balance the blocks. Count blocks in each bucket. Let children hypothesize why one bucket has more blocks than the other. Weigh and compare toys.

- Use vocabulary related to time when discussing the schedule of the day. Point to the clock and tell children, "We will have lunch when the big and little hands of the clock are on the twelve." Point out the numerals on a digital clock and relate them to activity segments.

- Use words such as "after," "before," and "in a few minutes" in discussions. It is difficult for young children to understand "five minutes" or "half an hour," but using the terms familiarizes them with the vocabulary. Many preschoolers know the time they get up in the morning and the time they go to bed. Some begin telling time.

PRESCHOOL ACTIVITIES

Provide Experiences That Use Counting

These are activities around the numeral 5. Use your creativity for other numerals!

- Invite children to take five crackers and five cheese tidbits for snack. Give three straight pretzels and two curly pretzels. Ask the child how many total pretzels she has. Count rocks or acorns on the playground and line them up in piles of five. Sort by size.

- Sing "Five Little Ducks." Select and count five children to act it out. Repeat the activity until all children have a turn. Recount using ordinal numbers ("first" through "fifth") instead of cardinal numbers. Write the numerals as part of a rebus of the song. Write the sequence that shows subtraction in each verse.

- Build all kinds of structures using only five blocks. Repeat with Legos, bristle blocks, colored blocks, or snap blocks.

- Plant five beans in a cup.

- Hop five times, jump five times, crawl five steps, and turn around five times.

- Count quietly, "One, two, three, four," and then say, "Five," in a loud voice. Repeat.

PRESCHOOL ACTIVITIES

Build Math Vocabulary

- Compare the shapes of crackers. Point out the number of sides or corners. Compare oval and round.

- Cut fruits, cheese slices, and vegetables into circles, rectangles, and triangles. Arrange a variety of food slices by size from largest to smallest or smallest to largest. Recategorize by shape; then arrange by color.

❯ Give children pretzel sticks to use to create different shapes on top of a spread on slices of bread. Compare how many pretzels different children used to make the same shape.

❯ Compare a large and small square book, pointing out that they have the same number of sides and corners. Discuss equal distances between all four sides and corners. Measure the books and compare the sizes. Arrange them from smallest to largest. Let the children predict which book has the most pages and which has the fewest: "Do all small books have the same number of pages?" Count to confirm. See how many books have different rectangular configurations. Compare measurements. Chart the findings.

❯ Cut fruits and vegetables with the children and use fractions as you compare the whole and parts (half,

quarter, fourth). Show how to reassemble pieces for an image of whole versus part. Do the same with other foods that you cut.

❯ Point out patterns on clothing or wallpaper: "Pink dot, pink dot, blue dot, pink dot, pink dot. What comes next?" "This duck is standing on its feet, and this duck is on its head. This duck is standing on its feet. What comes next?"

❯ Arrange leaves and sticks in a pattern and help children figure out what comes first and what comes next. Remove one item from the middle of the pattern and ask the children to identify what is missing.

❯ Without counting, have the children divide into groups based on the colors of their shirts or the type of shoes they are wearing. Help them estimate which group is the largest or smallest. Count to confirm the answer.

- Have each child gather leaves, rocks, or sticks. Ask who they think has the most and the least and which children gathered about the same amount; then count.

- Have a race. See who is first, second, or last. Change the activity to hopping or skipping.

- Compare different kinds of spiders and different size spiders as you sing Raffi's "There's a Spider on the Wall." Make your movements coincide with the size as you act out the song. Compare the size of spiders to other animals using size comparison vocabulary, such as "smaller," "larger," "tiny," or "huge."

Building Math Vocabulary in the Discovery Area

- "How many fish are in the tank?"

- "Who can find three things that float?"

- "You and Millie look the same size. Why don't you measure each other?"

- "What shape is the bird's egg?"

Building a Math Vocabulary in the Block Area

- "Which part of the building used the most blocks?"

- "You built two towers. Which is taller?"

- "You made a symmetrical building. Look, this side and this side used the same number of blocks."

- "Let's see how many triangular blocks you used to create that doorway. Help me count."

- "Which ball do you think will reach the bottom of the ramp first?"

- "Select a train car to go between the engine and the caboose."

Build Math Vocabulary in the Dramatic Play Area

- "How many plates will you need to feed your children?"

- "Mr. Shoemaker, how much do these shoes cost to repair?"

- "Can you find six hats, one for each of the babies?"

- "We need more chairs so everyone can sit on the bus. How many more will we need from the other side of the room?"

- "What time will you put your doll to bed?"

Build Math Vocabulary in the Art Area

- "What two shapes did you use to make that design?"

- "Let's count how many pieces of material you pasted on the paper plate."

- "There are only enough pom-poms for each child to have two. How many pom-poms do we have?"

- "These three stripes are vertical, and these four stripes are horizontal. Let's count to see how many stripes you painted."

- "Select the color of paint you want to use first."

Music, Cognition, and the Brain

Ten children sit quietly and listen to Mozart's "Eine Kleine Nachtmusik." Another group of children join the teacher in doing the "Hokey Pokey." Which group is learning more? Does one group use more parts of the brain? Early publicity on brain research cited information on the positive effects of listening to Mozart, which is thought to have the most complex musical counterpoint of all music. After listening to Mozart, college students temporarily did better on the Stanford-Binet Intelligence Scale. These findings led to an explosion of the use of Mozart music with the notion that listening to classical music made children smarter. Listening to Mozart *cannot* raise a child's IQ! However, it is probable that listening to complex music builds more complex neural networking (Shore 2002).

Does one kind of music have an effect on the brain that is better or worse than another kind of music? No studies have definitively answered this question. Since music and emotions are closely related, loud music may stimulate some children and create behavior problems. That said, music can also be used to help children relax and may help them focus. Music engages the same pathways used for problem solving and mathematical skills, but just listening to music will not make a child smarter.

The brain differs in how it responds to listening to music and creating music. When playing the piano, more senses are used than when listening to the piano. The child strikes keys (tactile), hears the notes (auditory), and sees the hands move on a keyboard (visual), which wires different neurons than just passively listening to music. Music lessons stimulate similar areas of the brain as mathematical tasks. Music may even strengthen connections between brain cells in the cortex (Sousa 2006).

Music sets the mood and helps bring focus and attention to learning. Start each day with a song containing words. Playing soft classical music as a background for learning centers might help children focus better and remain calm as they play. End the day with a happy, fun song.

Listen to a variety of music with children, and point out high and low notes or fast and slow tempo to develop listening skills. Adding words to music aids language acquisition. The rhythm of music helps put the words from the music into permanent memory (Jensen 2005). Songs teach the rhyme, rhythm, and cadence of spoken language.

PRESCHOOL ACTIVITIES

Find Alternate Ways to Use Familiar Songs

"Twinkle, Twinkle, Little Star"

> Sing the song alone or with hand motions.

> Sing other songs with the same tune, such as the "ABC Song" or "Little Arabella Miller."

> Sing the song in rounds.

> Sing the song using words about other things besides stars that twinkle, such as headlights, flashlights, or lightning bugs.

> Turn off most lights. Give each child a flashlight to turn on and off while singing.

"If You're Happy and You Know It"

> Sing with hand motions and no words. Hum the tune or sing "la, la."

> Make up new verses and use other actions. Hop on one foot, jump up and down, or shake a friend's hand.

> Sing other songs with the same tune, such as "Put Your Finger in the Air."

> Turn two groups of children so they are sitting back-to-back. Assign a child to be the group leader. Each group sings, seeing only the leader of their song. Sing two different songs with the same tune at the same time.

"She'll Be Coming 'Round the Mountain"

> Act out the story as you sing.

> Change horses to motorcycles, race cars, or rocket ships. Help children make up new verses.

- Make a rebus of the song using poster board and pictures of some of the words (mountains, white horses, waving hands, and chicken and dumplings).

"Yankee Doodle"

- Have the children clap their hands on their legs, galloping to the tune.

- Have several children act out the song as other children sing. Switch roles so everyone gets a turn acting and singing.

- Play rhythm instruments as you sing. Divide children into two groups so some play instruments on the first line and others play on the second. Have all children play during the chorus.

- Choose one word that no one sings during the song. Everyone claps instead of singing the word. "Yankee (clap) went to town a-riding on a pony."

PRESCHOOL ACTIVITIES

Support Musical Enrichment

- Chant as well as sing songs, such as "Miss Mary Mack" by Ella Jenkins or "Humpty Dumpty" by Thomas Moore.

- Play songs with lyrics that give specific movement directions. Al Rasso, Hap Palmer, and Ella Jenkins have songs with easy-to-follow movement activities.

- Act out songs, such as "Polly Had a Dolly" or "Hush, Little Baby."

- Sing a song with rhyming words. List other rhyming words that could be substituted.

- Sing, act out, and then compare the monkeys in two songs: "Five Monkeys Jumping on the Bed" and "Five Monkeys Swinging in the Trees." "Five Little Ducks" and "One Little Duck with the Feather on His Back" Find other songs with the same animals, and compare their descriptions and actions. List similarities and differences. Act out the two songs.

- Use hand and body motions while singing Raffi's "The Wheels on the Bus." Change the song to "The People at the Park" and add action verbs to get children up and moving.

- Change "Itsy Bitsy Spider" to the great-big or middle-size spider. Use different pitches of voice to reflect the spider's size.

- Discuss musical intonation when singing familiar songs.

- Make up tunes of simple facts, such as phone numbers and addresses that you want children to memorize. Music speeds up the memory process.

- Link art and music by having children draw or paint to music and describe music in "color words."

- Experiment with different rhythms.

- Help children create their own tunes to accompany their activities.

- Change the lyrics of "Row, Row, Row Your Boat" to "Drive, Drive, Drive the Car," or "Go Up, Up, Up the Stream." Think of new verses.

- Read illustrated songbooks. Some examples include *Twinkle, Twinkle, Little Star*, *Old MacDonald Had a Farm*, or *Baby Beluga* by Raffi. Show children the pictures as well as the words that match the lyrics they are singing. *Boom Chicka Rock* by John Archambault combines words and music to create a story.

PRESCHOOL ACTIVITIES

Use Musical Instruments

- Use drums, sand blocks, and tambourines while singing "Johnny Works with One Hammer."

- Use triangles, tambourines, kazoos, wood blocks, and rhythm sticks to accompany culturally diverse music. Teach children to play fast, slow, high, low, loud, and soft. Add steel drums or a rain stick.

- Follow the directions of Ella Jenkins's songs "Play Your Instruments" and "Put Your Instruments Away."

- Clap out the rhythm of a song; then use rhythm instruments to accent the cadence.

- Visit a high school band or orchestra class. Listen to one instrument at a time. Let the children touch the instrument and feel the vibrations as it is played.

- Borrow a used instrument from a music store. Let the children explore. Try to have a different instrument each month. Let children experiment after you establish rules, and make sure instruments with mouthpieces are sanitized between children. This activity requires good supervision.

- Listen to musical stories, such as "Tubby the Tuba," "Fantasia," and "Peter and the Wolf."

- Let children put handbells in sequence from high to low pitch or low to high.

- Play classical music for active listening. Point out the sounds of the drum, flute, or piano as they are played. Have books or pictures of instruments available while listening to music.

- Pantomime the action of instruments being played as the children listen to music.

- Listen to a variety of culturally diverse music styles.

- Purchase bongo and African drums for children to hold and play. Help each child create an original drum song. Repeat short and complicated patterns played on the drum.

- Make drums from coffee or oatmeal containers and kazoos from paper towel rolls (use a rubber band to cover one end with wax paper and make a small hole in the wax paper; children hum or sing loudly into the tube from the uncovered side). Assemble a kitchen band with homemade drums, kazoos, cymbals, and pots and pans, and play the instruments in a parade.

- Invite adults or older children to play instruments. Give children time to experiment with the school's instruments, such as a piano, guitar, or autoharp.

- Help children learn the different pitches on a keyboard. Sing along using a very high or very low voice. Establish rules of use for the keyboards.

- Play a rhythm instrument and have a child whose eyes are closed guess which instrument made the sound or pitch. Have children guess the tune played on a kazoo or keyboard.

Creative Movement

Moving creatively to music coupled with words not only helps children understand the tempo of music and the beat of speech but also stimulates several parts of the brain at the same time. Children learn to move to the words or to the music. Each child should be allowed to interpret the movement, allowing for many differences as they clap, bend, sway, or jump. Thinking and moving together is a skill. To prevent injuries, be sure the area is large enough for each child to move freely. This is a fun activity and helps children move in conjunction with other children. It also provides good exercise and is a nice transition during group time.

Support Creative Movement

❯ Use a variety of music that has different rhythms. Provide ribbons and scarves, and encourage children to create their own movement to express the music.

❯ After reading *The Giving Tree* by Shel Silverstein, put on classical music and encourage children to sway with the wind. Vary the tempo so the wind blows hard and softly.

❯ Pretend to be flames of a candle. Let a child blow as the candle flames move and then are extinguished.

❯ Move like animals, transportation vehicles, or insects. Use vocabulary associated with the movement: ducks waddle, fish swim, horses gallop.

❯ Sing "The Little Gray Ponies" as the children gallop, jump fences, and sleep like ponies.

❯ Give each child two paper plates. Clap them together, twirl them, and shake them from side to side as music plays.

❯ Create silly movement patterns that the children can follow. Have children take turns being the leader.

❯ Stand in a circle. Have one child create a movement, such as stamping a foot or clapping hands, and have everyone copy it. Change leaders often.

❯ Spin like a top, grow like a flower, or jump like jumping beans.

❯ Move like monkeys or alligators as you recite the poem "Five Little Monkeys Swinging in the Tree."

❯ Play music. Let each child choose a movement that the music suggests as they dance, clap, jump, or skip to reach their destination across the room.

CLOSING THOUGHTS

Each child needs a variety of experiences and a multitude of activities that are meaningful to form the foundations for learning. They are like a pearl in an oyster. In the beginning, there is a grain of sand or knowledge. Each time the child experiences interaction with the object or experiments with the concept, a layer of understanding forms around the beginning idea. Just as the oyster adds layer upon layer of mineral to form the pearl, the child adds perceptions, understanding, and impressions that help clarify and define ideas. The learning builds layer by layer, each adding to the next. The result is a pearl of wisdom embedded in memory. Since people don't ever stop learning, the layers continue to build throughout their lifetimes.

The next chapter covers the language skills that preschoolers develop in correlation with the learning that occurs when they play and interact in an enriched setting. Climbing the ladder to proficiency, the child builds on the knowledge he has and uses his thought processes to foster language. The communication skills the child learns through a variety of activities and experiences are necessary for emergent literacy.

chapter 8

Emergent Literacy in Preschoolers

Preschool children's ability to talk with an ever-expanding vocabulary allows them to more easily communicate with others. Their sentences have a recognizable structure. They can make statements, ask questions, and put together ideas in a coherent conversation. Even though preschool children demonstrate increased language proficiency, they still need teachers and parents to intentionally create an environment full of activities that advance their language skills. Each day children build language competency on top of the foundation they created in their first few years. At three, four, and five years old, they are ready to ascend the ladder of knowledge that requires refined communication skills and leads to reading and writing.

Children's literacy development is a continuous process that begins in infancy with exposure to oral language, books and stories, and written language. Fill the environment with print, read many books, and demonstrate writing. Play with language and literacy in a variety of ways. Help children experience the joy and power of learning the basic concepts of print, which lead to reading and writing. You will thereby help children become successful readers in future years.

THE CAREGIVER'S ROLE

Provide a print-rich environment that exposes children to printed words in a variety of ways throughout the day. Do not clutter the room with too many labels. Only put print where the words have a purpose and meaning in the environment (Copple and Bredekamp 2009). Make signs to augment play. When children create a bus from chairs, write the word "bus," to add to the fantasy. Label block constructions. Erect signs that give directions: "Swings closed today" or "Save this block building." Generate lists for groceries, activities for the day, names of absent children, or names of children waiting for a turn at a popular learning center, and write them on chalkboards or large pieces of chart paper.

Modeling writing is important. Children want to copy the adults in their lives. As they watch adults write and then read back what has been written, all the squiggly lines take on meaning. Children are exposed to left to right organization and see that the symbols represent words (Pitcher, Feinburg, and Alexander 2000). You can help children learn many print features: that print has meaning and tells a story, that multiple letters followed by spaces are words, and that printed words correspond with spoken words (NAEYC and IRA 2005). When reading stories, point to beginning and ending letters and words. Show children the same word throughout the story. You'll be teaching *word awareness*. Helping children see the similarities and differences in letters by comparing shapes is important. Show them the difference between the number of letters in a short word and in a long word. Provide alphabet books, magnetic letters, and alphabet puzzles for children to manipulate and experiment with letter combinations (NAEYC and IRA 2005). Provide children with many opportunities to express their ideas on paper. Help children understand that writing has a real purpose. In the beginning, accept scribbles and creative spelling as writing. This will give children the confidence to try to write their ideas.

PRELITERACY SKILLS

Learning to read and write does not come naturally. Unlike with spoken language, children do not just pick up these skills by being surrounded by people who can read and write. First, children have to learn that spoken language and written words are connected. They begin to understand the function of printed materials and the form they are in by having many experiences with books and written

language. They have to understand how books open, which side of the page to read first, and when print is upside down. They have to learn to move their eyes from left to right to read a sentence, and they have to obtain a level of hand-eye coordination to write letters and words. Their fine-motor skills have to mature until they can control a writing implement or select keys on a computer. Children have to understand combined sounds in order to read and write. They have to learn that letters are not randomly placed, but that there is an order of consonants and vowels that creates words. They have to understand that letters represent words and that by arranging the letters differently, other words can be created. Words also have to be placed in a specific order to create a sentence. Learning preliteracy skills is abstract, and the brain has to have many synaptic connections garnered from many experiences before a child is ready to read or write.

How does this happen? Part of literacy competence relies on muscle maturation. The brain connections between motor and cognitive areas have to develop through many different types of experiences to allow the child to put her thoughts into written words. The child's coordination has to go from grasping a pencil to being able to write a letter or number. Young children do not learn to read and write by sitting down and listening to lectures on grammar, word placement, letter recognition, or other reading and writing skills. Instead, you must provide a myriad of experiences linked to literacy. Language and communication skills are intertwined in everything young children do during the preschool experience. Being immersed in a literacy-rich environment allows children to move through the early, or preliteracy, stages toward becoming literate. Here are some things to keep in mind:

- Talk with children and encourage them to talk with others.

- Listen to children and encourage them to listen to others.

- Help children develop a love of books.
  - Read a variety of fiction and nonfiction books in a safe, comfortable atmosphere.

- Establish a routine of reading a story before and after naps, as a calming time after outdoor play, and as a special treat before going home.

- Choose books you like. Children can sense when adults value literature and enjoy reading to them.

- Vary the books and the language used as needed for the age of the child or children you are reading to.

• Provide culturally relevant language experiences.

• Encourage children to express themselves in a variety of ways.

• Help children build vocabulary.

• Expose children to a variety of books, and help them develop print knowledge.

• Support children in their home languages as they acquire English language skills.

Reading Every Day

It's important to read often to children to advance their literacy skills. Plan to read a minimum of two stories a day. Reading more books daily is advantageous. Children learn the cadence and rhythm of spoken language when they hear books being read. They also learn print literacy. In addition to books, let children see you read letters, notes, charts, and posters. Create a print-rich environment throughout the day. Let them see and begin to understand that specific kinds of marks (letters) have meaning. Children learn to read the visual cues in pictures near the print and understand that the words describe the picture. Children begin to process letters, translate them into sounds, and connect this information with a known meaning as the first step toward alphabetic understanding (NAEYC and IRA 2005). They learn what is the top and bottom of a book, how to turn pages, and how to get clues from pictures. They can be shown left-to-right sequencing and may begin to move their eyes along the print line.

Children who are read to often do not read earlier than other children. However, they may do better scholastically. The early wiring of the brain gives them a firm advantage. Children often ask for the same book over and over. This repetition helps them make the connections in their brains more permanent and puts the words, sounds, and rhythm of the words into memory. Children love to hear the repetition. An important step in the literacy process occurs when children know a book so well that they can tell if any portion of the text has been skipped. They can retell the story and even memorize word groups.

Millions of Cats by Wanda Gág and *Caps for Sale* by Esphyr Slobodkina are predictable books that repeat a verse of rhyme throughout the story. Children quickly learn the repeated portion and are able to help tell the story. Another kind of predictable story is one where an item is added from time to time with a review of all that has gone on before. *Green Eggs and Ham* by Dr. Seuss or *I Know an Old Lady Who Swallowed a Fly* are in that category. Children hear the list repeated until it enters into working memory. The ability to remember and repeat the predictable portion or memorizing the entire story is another important step in reading readiness. Through repetition, children master not only the plot, but also the sequence of the story line and much of the vocabulary. Thus, predictable books that repeat a section over and over are fun to read and reinforce brain connections.

PRESCHOOL ACTIVITIES

Promote Literacy with Books and Pictures

❯ Read the book with lots of animation and expression in your voice. Read the pictures as well as the words. Let children learn to love the sound of your voice as you read. Help them listen to the rhythm and cadence of language. Encourage imitation.

❯ Look at a picture from a magazine. Help the child create a story about the picture. Attach the written story to the picture.

- Don't always try to use story time as a teaching moment. Make reading a joy.

- Stop occasionally and let the children add the next word as the book becomes more familiar.

- Before reading a new book, let the children predict from the cover or a picture what the book is about. Read a portion and ask what will happen next before you turn the page. Since the children don't know the story, their answers are always correct. Read the book and compare the predictions with the actual story.

- Help the children find the missing person or describe the action on the page in books without words. *Where's Waldo* by Martin Handford or *Nothing Ever Happens on My Block* by Ellen Raskin are fun and can spark imaginary plots.

- Help children see a repeated word by pointing out the word's shape and letter sequencing.

- Show words that begin with the same letter. Sound out letters and the word.

- Emphasize words that rhyme. Generate a list of other words that rhyme. Allow made up words too!

- Let children imagine what happened before or after the printed story. Their answers are always correct.

- Compare two books with similar characters. Compare the wolf in *Little Red Riding Hood* and the wolf in *Three Little Pigs*. How are they the same? How are they different?

- Compare two editions of the same folktale, such as *Little Red Riding Hood* or *The Three Billy Goats Gruff*. Compare the pictures of the characters and the set of adventures. Make lists of similarities and differences.

- Ask very few questions about the plot to assess comprehension. Often this is the only extension teachers and parents provide for a story. Try to discuss ideas instead.

- Ask open-ended questions about the plot to spur children's thinking skills and creativity: "How long do you think it took each pig to build its house?" There are no right or wrong answers. Accept all the children's suggestions.

- Provide audio books along with the printed book. Access e-books with audio on the Internet or on mobile multitouch devices. Add headphones for independent listening. Invite families to record favorite stories and add them to the listening center.

- Cook along with a story to enhance understanding of the tale as well as to stimulate both taste and smell, which activates multiple areas of the brain. Prepare green scrambled eggs after reading *Green Eggs and Ham* by Dr. Seuss, bake blueberry muffins after hearing *Blueberries for Sale* by Robert McCloskey, or bake bread after hearing *Tony's Bread* by Tomie DePaola to add excitement, motivation, and fun.

Spoken Language

Being surrounded by spoken language is enough for children not only to learn words but also to replicate sentence formation, nouns, verb tenses, adjectives, and pronouns. Children learn to speak the same language they hear. While children are learning, they make mistakes in both pronunciation and grammar. Most children pick up the spoken language of their surroundings and can self-correct. The window of opportunity for acquiring spoken language is the first four years. These years should be filled with lots of talking, reading, singing, and word games. Some children need specific intervention from a speech therapist to help them acquire language skills in addition to being immersed in a language-rich environment.

Fingerplays

Fingerplays give children an opportunity to talk and move simultaneously. Add thinking skills by switching themes of familiar fingerplays. Point out the rhyming words, or help children think of new ones at the end of each sentence. Use chants, fingerplays, and nursery rhymes daily. Rehearsal increases memory. When you add hand and body motions, you are helping children use multiple

- *Alexander and the Terrible, Horrible, No Good, Very Bad Day* by Judith Viorst

- *Tikki Tikki Tembo* by Arlene Mosel

- *The Funny Little Woman* by Arlene Mosel

- *The Poky Little Puppy* by Janette Sebring Lowrey

- *We're Going on a Bear Hunt* by Michael Rosen and Helen Oxenbury

- *Aesop's Fables* and other folktales

PRESCHOOL ACTIVITIES

Support Storytelling

❯ Let children retell a story in their own words. Record their original story and listen to it. Discuss differences from the book.

❯ Take a well-known story and write a class version with the children picking the adventures. *Yuk Soup* and *Mrs. Wishy-Washy*, both by Joy Crowley, are easy to rewrite.

❯ Read *Three Little Pigs*; then invite children to retell it with different characters. Perhaps their story would be about the *Three Little Lambs*. *The Very Hungry Caterpillar* by Eric Carle can become *The Very Hungry Tadpole*. Write a child-generated story on poster board and put it in the library area.

❯ Read a familiar story out loud as the children act it out.

❯ Tell a story where the gingerbread man chases the people or animals and tries to make them play with him. Let the children create reasons why they should stop or not stop.

❯ Choose new foods as you read the story *Cloudy with a Chance of Meatballs* by Judi Barrett and Ronald Barrett. Get creative and have only sweets or only healthy foods fall from the sky. Guess which animal climbs on the raft next in *There's Always Room for One More* by Ingrid and Dieter Schubert by telling

parts of the brain at the same time. The rhythm and cadence of chants and nursery rhymes help create memories of speech patterns.

Storytelling

Storytelling is a different way to present a tale. There are no pictures, so children can create their own visual images, sparking their imaginations. Dramatization will hold the child's attention if your voice and pitch changes with each character. Eye contact and body movements improve the performance. Storytelling enhances listening skills and is especially useful when riding in a car or bus or waiting for a meal or snack.

Flannel board stories are a variation of storytelling. Purchase flannel board stories or make your own by taking books in poor condition and recycling the pictures. Secure felt or Velcro onto the back of pictures. Tell the story as you manipulate the flannel board figures. After you have told the story several times, let the children move the figures as they try to recreate the tale. The following are good titles to engage children in telling stories:

- *Ming Lo Moves the Mountain* by Arnold Lobel

- *Sylvester and the Magic Pebble* by William Steig

riddles for each and then showing the picture. Substitute community workers for animals.

❯ Change calling a dog to clapping for a cat or tweeting to imitate a bird in *Whistle for Willie* by Ezra Jack Keats. See which children can whistle at the beginning of the year and write a story about the children in the group who can and those who are still trying to whistle. Check who can whistle at the end of the year and rewrite the story.

❯ Gather many books that have one type of animal, such as dogs, and compare the attributes. Compare the illustrations in the book with actual pictures of the dogs.

❯ Read, and reread, books by one author for a week or two and collect information about the author's life. Clarify the difference between being an author, an illustrator, and a publisher.

❯ Using chart paper, write a story as a group about the adventures of a small toy. Teach children that stories have a beginning, a middle, and an end. Begin with three sentences only. Decide on a title after writing the story. After the children are familiar with the process, the story can be made longer.

Building Vocabulary

Teachers often stand back and observe as children explore. This is important at times, but descriptive language needs to be brought into the play. The more complex language there is in a child's environment, the more sophisticated the child's language skills will be. When you use more words, an ever-changing vocabulary, and longer sentences, children develop more advanced language skills. These skills usually last a lifetime (Shore 2002). The amount of language a child hears influences the child's emerging language skills and vocabulary acquisition. Caregivers must be verbal around young children all day long. It is important not only to describe their play using task-centered talking but also to ask open-ended questions as children become more verbal. Explain, hypothesize, and "think out loud." This exposes children to a rich

vocabulary. The following are some vocabulary-building activities in specific interest areas:

• Use words to communicate needs and plans to others.

• Learn about whole and part.

• Acquire vocabulary words associated with blocks, dramatic play, science, water and sand, and other interest areas.

• Name pictures or create a story around an art creation.

• See adults write dictation on paper.

• Use words to communicate needs to others.

• Make up a story as the plot is acted out.

• Plan and articulate activities.

• Use words to communicate observations to others.

Adults can reinforce vocabulary development and language skills while children work in interest areas.

PRESCHOOL ACTIVITIES

Build Vocabulary in All Areas

❯ "I'll help you write a warning that the driveway is steep. What do you want the sign to say?"

❯ "Look into the microscope at the crystal."
"What do you think caused the water to evaporate?"
"The algae in the water make it look murky."

❯ "Leonardo, would you like to write your new puppy's name on the back of his picture?"

❯ "Those shoes you are wearing are used for dancing and are called ballet slippers."

❯ "What are your restaurant specials tonight?"

❯ "Are you the appliance repairman? Our stove is broken."

> "How did you make this unusual color?" "You made a new color from the green and blue. It is turquoise."

> "Can you tell me a story about your drawing? I'll write the words."

> "Ask Angela to please pass you the scissors."

> "Alexandra will like the get-well card you made for her. You wrote both her name and yours. Here is an envelope to put it in. After we put her address on it, we can take it to the office to be mailed."

> "You put your name on this form and lots of letters on the lines. Here is an envelope to put it in so you can take it home."

Communication Skills

Learning how to discuss and communicate comes with practice. Lots of rich vocabulary will arise in group and one-on-one discussions. Children learn syntax and grammar in a relaxed atmosphere. Children will practice the give-and-take of a conversation. Model active listening skills and making eye contact with others. Make sure the discussion is something the children are interested in talking about. Keep discussions short to match attention spans. Reviewing information the child learned through self-discovery strengthens brain connections and helps the child retain the information. The child uses information from her memory to add previously learned information to the topic being discussed. Let the child explain what he has experienced relevant to the topic. It will help the child move the information into working memory and eventually into permanent memory.

The quantity of interactions a child has with an adult during communication also has an effect on language achievement. Parents may lengthen a conversation with a very young child, allowing for an interplay of ideas back and forth, whereas the child care provider may end it due to the obligations of teaching a group. In the example that follows the number of interactions with the parent is higher than what the teacher provides.

Parent: We are out of bread.
Child: Why?
Parent: Because we used it up at lunch.
Child: Why?
Parent: Because everyone wanted a piece of bread.
Child: Why?
Parent: Because we all like bologna sandwiches. We'll get more bread when we go to the store.
Child: Why?
Parent: Because we need to buy bread and milk.
Child: Why?
Parent: I don't have any milk. Do you want water or juice with your crackers?

Caregiver: We are out of bread.
Child: Why?
Caregiver: Because we used it up at snacktime.
Child: Why?
Caregiver: It is time to sit down and eat your lunch.

Since caring for a group of children restricts the amount of time you have with each child, extend the conversation at a later time. Sitting and talking with children as a family during snack- and mealtimes contributes to building vocabulary and learning proper grammar. The caregiver can complete the scenario: "I was telling Jimmy that we are out of bread. Does anybody know why?" Treating this like a discussion will help children think critically, an important learning tool.

PRESCHOOL ACTIVITIES

Increase Communication Skills

> Gather information from street and building signs in the children's surroundings.

> Collect information from nonverbal body language.

> Get consensus on rules for the playground equipment.

- Discuss multiple ways to use a new manipulative toy.

- Let children decide on foods as they plan a class lunch or party.

- Pick, feel, and discuss leaves from the garden or a nature walk. Note their differences. Together, look in books or on the Internet for specific information about the leaves. Extend this by having children bring in leaves from trees and bushes from home to compare.

- Begin research on pets, favorite foods, and clothing patterns, such as polka dots or plaids. Find out each child's preferences.

- Make any interest of the children into a short discussion. Topics could include weather, animals, toys, special events, or music.

- Begin a story and let the children finish it.

- Make up a round-robin story.

- Have young children dictate stories and picture descriptions for you to write out. Keep a journal for each child.

The Writing Table

In addition to the learning areas covered in chapter 7, every early childhood classroom needs a writing table. Children should be encouraged to write notes to their friends and family. The following are ideas for ways to add interest to the writing area:

- Supply all sizes of pencils, crayons, and markers. Some children prefer the larger, fat barrels; others have more control with slim barrels.

- Include a variety of sizes and types of paper. Include notepads and plain and lined paper. Carbonless copy paper allows children to write on the top layer and see the marks on subsequent pages. Used checkbooks, office memo pads, restaurant order forms, stationery, and envelopes inspire writing.

- Use pencil boxes to house skinny markers, various colored pens, and a variety of pencils, including colored pencils.

- Get a box with dividers from a grocery store and turn it into shelves for each kind of writing implement.

- Add stickers for pretend stamps, used or new greeting cards, and weekly readers or newspapers for young children to use.

- Ask businesses and parents to donate a variety of recycled paper, paper pads, spiral notebooks, and forms.

- Include a stamp pad and alphabet stamps to add interest. The theme can be changed to go along with classroom themes. After a field trip, children can be encouraged to write thank-you notes to the host or parents who chaperoned.

- Provide magnetic and wooden letters for children to manipulate.

- Put sand into shallow pans and let children "write" using their fingers. Use fingerpaint to practice letters and words.

- Supply chalkboards, which are exciting to use and offer children a large surface to write their beginning letters. Erasing the product is just as much fun as writing.

- Supply blank forms to fill out and envelopes to address.

- Add an alphabet chart on a nearby wall or index cards with one letter on each to help children see how letters are formed.

- Save child-appropriate greeting cards and magazines to add to the area. Incorporate holiday greetings cards or holiday paper to coincide with upcoming dates.

- Make calendars available for children to write in special events.

- Add old envelopes—ask families to save ones from advertisements that come in the mail.

Do not include all of these supplies at once. Organize the items so children will not be overwhelmed. As in other areas of the classroom, the writing table should be kept neat and children taught how to put away the supplies before leaving the area.

Literacy Prop Boxes

Literacy props can be added to other prop boxes or used to created stand-alone literacy prop boxes. The boxes can include books, puppets, and magazine articles. Always have paper and pencils available when using prop boxes. Change prop boxes for the writing table frequently and include themes around holidays, field trips, or community helpers. You can focus on one animal, one story, or one author. Create a prop box around any favorite book. Look for props that are described in the story. After reading the book many times, children can re-create their own version of the story.

PRESCHOOL ACTIVITIES

Use Literacy Prop Boxes

❯ Read *The Story of the Three Bears*. Supply three different size toy bears to represent the mother, father, and baby. Add three bowls, spoons, and carpet squares to serve as beds with three blankets. Put the box near three chairs in the room. The story can be acted out then dictated by the children and written down by an adult. Place various versions of the book in the box. Compare the story lines and pictures for similarities and differences.

❯ Read *The Very Hungry Caterpillar* by Eric Carle. Collect various large, plastic fruits, a toy caterpillar, and a butterfly puppet. Encourage children to dictate their own version of the story. Bake cookies with holes in them. Children can decorate half of a paper towel roll to be transformed into a chrysalis that will hold a tissue-paper butterfly used in retelling the story. The story can be acted out. New versions of the story can be created with different foods.

❯ Read *The Three Little Kittens*. For props, use stuffed kittens, flannel board kittens or kitten puppets, a toy mouse, three sets of mittens, a clothesline, a plastic pie, three plastic plates, and a washtub with a scrub board. Children can act out the story, dictate it to a teacher, or tell it to other children.

❯ Read *The Grouchy Ladybug* by Eric Carle. Assemble puppets or stuffed animals of the ladybug, insects, and animals from the story. Act out the story. Read nature books about ladybugs. Order ladybugs from 1-800-LIVEBUG. Observe them before releasing them outside. Cut apples in half and use two pretzels for antenna and enjoy a ladybug snack. Provide red and black paint and invite children to paint ladybugs. Discuss the feelings the ladybug had at the beginning of the story and compare them to the feelings at the end of the story.

❯ Have a children's book series in a box. Compare plots and pictures of each book in the series. Here are some favorite series:

- Curious George by Margret Rey and H. A. Rey
- Harry the Dirty Dog by Gene Zion
- Frances by Russell Hoban
- The Berenstain Bears by Stan Berenstain and Jan Berenstain
- Frog and Toad by Arnold Lobel

- If You Give a Mouse a Cookie by Laura Joffe Numeroff

- Franklin by Paulette Bourgeois and Brenda Clark

➤ Post office: Provide paper, pencils, envelopes, pens, stickers for stamps, large purses for delivering letters, and a box with multiple dividers to sort mail. Encourage children to write letters and place them in the "mail box." Other children play mail carrier and deliver the letters to cubbies.

➤ Toy store: Place a variety of toys on shelves. Add prices and signs. Use cash registers, play money, and bags. Try other retail stores too. A flower shop, bakery, or gift store all make fun play areas.

➤ Food delivery service: Make picture menus. Add toy foods, bags, hats, toy phones, pens, and order forms. Some restaurants will give you props to use.

Learning a Second Language

Learning a second language is more easily accomplished in the first ten years than as a teen or adult. When young children are immersed in an environment with two languages, they can learn both. Children can be taught many foreign words through conversation and song. Repeating these words in other situations reinforces the brain's connections, helping to solidify the learning. For the words to be remembered, the use of the words must make sense and have meaning to the children. Substituting the Spanish or French word for an English word in the daily routine, during a story, or in a well-known song helps familiarize the children with words of other languages.

Second languages can be taught early yet must be done in developmentally appropriate ways. Having a weeklong theme on Mexico and learning Spanish words that are not repeated after the unit is over lacks the rehearsal and repetition needed for long-term memory. The words are soon forgotten. The Spanish words have to be incorporated into the daily routine for them to be moved into permanent memory. Songs and activities using multiple languages are fun and exciting to young children

and stimulate many parts of the brain at the same time, increasing memory capacity.

PRESCHOOL ACTIVITIES

Support Second-Language Acquisition

➤ Begin using a phrase or words from a second language along with the children's native language in situations where the children can derive meaning from the action or situation. Instead of always saying "friend," use the word "amigo" for a boy and "amiga" for a girl: "Kenya, pick an amiga to hold hands with as we walk to the playground. The child understands the meaning of the word in the context of the sentence.

➤ Listen to a native speaker part of every day. Infuse part of the culture into daily practice.

➤ Eat ethnic foods, use the proper terminology, and talk about the country of origin.

➤ Listen to familiar stories read in another language. Hearing *The Story of the Three Bears* in a different language is fascinating. Make sure the book has lots of pictures and is short to keep the children's attention. Point out the flow of words and the different sounds as it is read.

➤ Sing the original version and then the English version of "Frère Jacques" (French), "Kumbaya" (African), or "La Cucaracha" (Spanish).

➤ Listen to recordings of children's songs in other languages.

➤ Learn to say, "Happy Birthday," "Hello," or "I Love You" in several languages.

➤ Use second-language words and expressions— such as "hola" or "ciao" for hello—every day.

LITERACY SKILLS

Children in language-rich environments have better linguistic skills, which may aid them in learning to read (Sousa 2006). What constitutes a language-rich environment? Interact with children, giving them a running dialogue of happenings—using task-centered talking. Children communicate with each other and the teacher using conversational flow. There are written words around the room that identify not only the interest areas, but also working labels, such as a chart with the birthdays of the children, a sign to hang on the door that announces naptime is in progress, or a list of songs the children like. There are labels on shelves identifying the children's materials. Children's names are written on storage cubbies, on their personal items, and on a folder for families to take home. There are books in the library corner, lots of paper and writing implements on a writing table, and experience charts that list science experiment steps, field trip adventures, and original creative stories. Language and written words are an integral part of the classroom. Children are surrounded by all the pleasures of talking, reading, and writing. This type of environment aids the children in acquiring literacy skills.

Every child has her own timetable to move from the preliteracy stage to emergent literacy. Children show you that they are ready to move into the next stage when they ask what a printed word says or attempt to write letters. Observant teachers foster this inquisitive request by adding different literary activities.

Reading

Reading is not innate like speaking. Just being exposed to print does not result in reading print. There are no specific areas of the brain dedicated to learning to read. Because the process is so complicated, scientists are trying to decipher the steps the brain goes through in learning to read. Abstract symbols represent sounds from spoken language. Reading depends on the skill of the child's spoken language and the ability to distinguish the different sounds and relate them to the symbols.

Just because a child is in a language-rich atmosphere does not guarantee that reading will come easily. Three parts of the brain are involved in reading:

- The eye sees the printed word and sends the signal to the visual processing area.

- The auditory processing area of the brain sounds out the word.

- The cortex connects the sound and the meaning of the word (Sousa 2006).

The task is very complicated. Learning to read comes easily to about 50 percent of children. The other 50 percent find learning to read difficult, and 20 to 30 percent of these children struggle to learn to read (Sousa 2006).

Phonemes are the sounds of spoken language. Children first hear small segments of speech sounds. For example "ma" is the phoneme in "mama." These sounds make up syllables and, when put together, create words. The more experience young children have with hearing words, the easier it becomes for them to differentiate the many components of speech. They are making thousands of connections within the brain, forming a rich network that later will connect the visual information to the sounds

they have heard. In addition to beginning letter identification, rhymes, and syllables, children must know phonemes before they can read. The child must hear the sounds and be able to reproduce them before the sounds can be matched to abstract symbols for reading to occur. They learn that the words they hear can be represented by letters or a string of letters. Word and sound games that use phonemes make this learning fun and strengthen the child's ability to hear sound differences. Playing with language is often natural for children. Children chant, "Anna anna fo fanna, fee fi fo fanna, annnna." Pick up on this self-initiated activity, reinforce it, and expand it. Repeat what the child says or continue the consonant or vowel play.

When to Start?

Beginning the reading process too early may be detrimental to some children. Piaget felt that until a child could draw a perfect triangle, the brain had not developed to the point that children should be taught to read. Allowing children to mature naturally, without having to review letters and write letters daily, may be more effective. Surrounding prereading children with a language and print-rich environment as they play is more valuable than drilling children on letter recognition.

Researchers have looked at elementary children who were academic underachievers. Many of the children came from an environment that drilled on letters and rote alphabet recitation in preschool. Children did not play in a rich environment that offered a variety of activities including prereading skill formation. When other children were learning literacy skills in kindergarten, these early learners were tired of the activity and were hard to motivate to learn to read. The children who spent hours tracing and drawing letters, drilling on beginning, middle, and ending sounds, and reciting alphabet letters when they were three and four years old became dependent on the teacher for knowledge. They did not acquire the skills to learn on their own. So, by third grade or fifth grade, they had run out of learned knowledge and did not know how to advance their own learning (Brazelton 2001). Pressure to write and identify letters early also contributed to lack of success (Elkind 2001b). Repeated failure in a reading or writing activity can be stressful for a child. Repeated negative feelings may cause the brain to solidify connections related to failure, which may set up the child to fail more often.

Recently, there has been a drive to force academics on young children. The idea that play is a waste of time and that later academic performance will depend on the acquisition of early reading skills is prevalent. These ideas are compelling early care and education providers to stress rote alphabet memorization, isolated letter recitation, and sight word recognition. Instead of looking at early literacy as building a foundation of language that later will influence a child's ability to read and write, they are drilling on the alphabet. Repetition changes the cortex of the brain; however, there is a difference between repetition and drill. The brain fatigues when the experience is too long or has the consistent pattern of repetition found in drill (Perry 2003). The child stops attending and thinks of other things. Beware of using flash cards to teach letters and sight words. Drills and skills learned in isolation are devoid of meaning.

Some teenagers who participated in an academic preschool have a different attitude toward reading than many who experienced a play environment. Many children from the developmental play program are spontaneous readers and seem more motivated to read than children who were drilled on letters and taught to read earlier (Elkind 2001b). Many early readers are not "taught" to read. They had a parent or relative that read to them, took them to the library, and discussed books. Children are motivated by a rich exposure to language and books and the special attention of a warm, caring adult (Elkind 2001a). Learning to read should be free of stress. Introduce phonics as a comfortable and fun experience tied to the literacy activity. While reading a book, stop to point to words or letters in a very informal way. Animate your voice and make the story come alive. Reading will become a favored activity.

Teaching Letters

Brain research is teaching us that language skills should be taught throughout the day, not at "language time." When a child needs to have his name on a picture, that is the logical and optimum time to work with the letters that spell out his name. This will have far more impact than sitting the child down and "teaching" how to form letters in his name at a specific time chosen by the teacher (Pitcher, Feinburg, and Alexander 2000). Look for the teachable moments. When a child finds a friend's missing toy, that is the time to show the child all the names on the cubbies and help the child locate the other child's name through letter recognition and sound discrimination. If children randomly draw jobs for putting away toys, you can point out the connection between the letters and the phonemes and the identifying sign in the area of the classroom. Pointing out the repetition of letters or names on experience charts will develop the child's interest. These spontaneous learning moments have meaning to the children and make sense to them. The information is provided in a stress-free, yet highly interesting, context.

PRESCHOOL ACTIVITIES

Create Opportunities to Recognize the Letter "B"

What follows are activities for the letter "B." Use your creativity for other letters!

❯ Point out the letter "B" in the storybook, in experience charts, and when writing names.

❯ Point out the letter on the name cards on children's cubbies. Use cards with the children's names to choose learning centers or games outdoors. Children who have a "B" in their names select the cards and pass them around the circle.

❯ Put all toys beginning with the letter "B" in the middle of the circle. Have each child pick a toy and tell something about the toy.

❯ Give everyone in the group a page from the newspaper that has grocery coupons that begin with the letter "B." Give them scissors to cut them out, and pin them on a bulletin board.

❯ Let children circle the letter "B" in newspapers or magazines. Focus on both uppercase and lowercase letters.

❯ Have groups of three children lie down and form a "B" with their bodies.

❯ Roll bread dough into the letter "B" and bake it.

Rebuses, Word Walls, and Word Boxes

Promote reading by using the *rebus* method. This is a technique that replaces key words in a song or story with pictures. You can easily make a poster of a nursery rhyme or song. In "Hickory Dickory Dock," substitute pictures for "mouse" and "clock," with the rest of the words spelled out. As you recite the nursery rhyme, point to the words and pictures. This helps children realize that there is a word made up of letters with spaces in between that represents the spoken words. This will help children to acquire knowledge of the alphabet, phonological awareness, letter-sound correspondence, and an awareness of print concepts.

Another way to advance emergent reading skills is to create a *word wall*. Display collections of words that have meaning to the children on a wall near the writing center. Use a combination of large capital and lowercase letters so children see words just as they are written in books and on signs around

the room. The words can come from experience charts, activities, books, and science experiments. Daily happenings dictate new words to add. Children are encouraged to manipulate the words and add pictures.

Children's *word boxes* are another technique in advancing literacy. Have the child decorate a shoe box and cut a large slit in the lid. The child chooses a word she would like to learn to read. Print the word on a strip of poster board or an index card. Let the child draw a picture on the back. During the day, the child can go through the words with an adult and, if she wants, copy the word in the writing center. Some children begin a sight-word vocabulary using a word box. After the child can identify numerous words, you can add verbs, nouns, and articles so she can make simple sentences: "Mommy is home." "Daddy is reading." "I like cartoons." "I like ice cream."

Writing

Writing skills are an outgrowth of spoken language. Children need to have the hand-eye coordination to make circles and lines that intersect. The brain has to coordinate both knowledge and physical movement. Fine-motor skills of the hands and fingers have to work in concert with the child's memory and ideas to select the words to communicate. It is a very complicated process. Many children are pressured to write their names at an early age. They may have the language skills and can identify and spell their names before they have the musculature to write out the letters. This can be frustrating to both adults and children. Children should not be pushed to write. When they are developmentally able, they will write.

Children need to move from scribbling to making purposeful shapes before they can write. Experimenting with paints, markers, crayons, scissors, clay, and playdough uses the required muscles and establishes the necessary brain connections. Writing should not be taught in isolation. When a child needs to identify his art product or a stop sign for the street he is building, he will have a need and the motivation to learn to write letters.

Experience Charts

A common group activity is an *experience chart*, which is a written diary of class projects, cooking tasks, special events, and new adventures. Multiple children dictate activities to the teacher, who lists a sequence of events. Children see adults using large chart paper translate spoken word into print. This gives meaning to the printed language. Small illustrations at the end of each sentence clarify and help children give meaning to the written words. Alternate the colors of each written sentence to help children distinguish one statement from the next. Beginning each sentence with the name of a child helps that child and others identify what she dictated. Let children help write their own names and illustrate experience charts. Scribbles are acceptable.

Writing experience charts after field trips, science experiments, or nature walks not only provides immediate review but also creates permanent records that can be reread periodically. Try to relate a past event with the recent task. An experience chart about cleaning the fish tank and the colors of the fish leads to reading *The Rainbow Fish* by Marcus Pfister. After writing about an adventure at the zoo, act like each animal and make animal noises. Read books about individual animals, such as *The Zoo Book* by Jan Pfloog, or *Curious George Visits the Zoo* by Margret Rey and H. A. Rey. Children enjoy sharing an experience chart that has their names on it with friends and family members.

Journals

Write journals for the children as they create their own stories. This begins before children have the ability to write. Children dictate ideas, imaginary stories, or descriptions of pictures and block structures as an adult writes down the words. Staple several pages of newsprint or other paper into a small booklet. Let the child decorate the front, writing his name in large, bold letters. Each day or week, have the child tell you a real occurrence or an imagined story. Have the child sit next to you so he sees the text from the correct angle. As you write the dictated words, repeat each word as you print it. Then read back to the child what is said and let the child illustrate it. Take care to write exactly what the child has said and not to edit it or change the words to make complete sentences. Then, when the child looks at the words and letters and repeats what was said, there will be correlation.

Writing about a drawing or painting extends the printed word into the art area. There is some disagreement from educators about whether you should write directly on a child's product or on a separate piece of paper that is later attached. Do whatever is comfortable for you. Older children will dictate long explanations or create stories. This same technique can be used in the block area as children either describe how they built their structures or create a story around the building. Attach photos of the structure to the description.

Wrap cereal or cracker boxes in brown paper from grocery bags. These will become the child's own book. Have the child dictate a story. Write it on paper that will fit on one side of the box. Let the child glue it to the box. The child can illustrate the other side with markers or crayons. Write the title on the spine and the author's name on the other side. Put the book in the library area. These fit nicely on window sills.

Send a stuffed animal, puppet, or toy home with one child along with a blank notebook and attached pen. Encourage the family to write about the adventures that the animal has with the family over the weekend. Let the child first verbalize the activities and then hear them repeated as the teacher reads the journal.

Initial Attempts at Writing

Before children write actual letters and words, they may make shapes and symbols that resemble words or write squiggly lines that look like cursive writing. Enable and encourage these first attempts by having writing implements available at all times. Often the first word a child attempts to write is his or her name. In the beginning it may only be the first letter. It is important to accept these attempts without trying to correct the initial effort. The child

will self-correct or ask for help at a later time. As children begin writing, they often use inventive spelling. Some children write backwards. Again, accepting these interesting inventions gives the child confidence and aids early literacy (NAEYC and IRA 2005).

Children understand from an early age the importance of words and are motivated to learn to write letters. In the *project approach*, children label, create signs, and document their experiences with written words. Help them express their questions, thought processes, and solutions by writing for the children and encouraging them to replicate the signs and the key words (Helm and Katz 2001). See the list of writing table supplies earlier in this chapter for ways to support children's early attempts at writing.

Computers, Multitouch Mobile Devices, and Literacy

Technology is a reality in children's lives. Children need to be comfortable using computers and other digital technology. Computers and multitouch mobile devices can be used inappropriately as digital dittos with all the inherent dangers of meaningless drill, or they can become a hub of socialization, exploration, and information. Set up the computer area with two or three chairs so several children can participate and take turns. As with any other sedentary activity, time should be limited. Use a kitchen timer that rings after fifteen minutes so

other children can have experience at the computer. Establish rules for use, such as no pounding on the keys.

Be actively involved, add relevant comments, and give help when needed. Plan to use the computer as a source of information. When children find an insect or plant, look up facts about it on the Internet and read the information to the children. Print out a picture to post. Write a caption about the object.

Interactive computer software programs and applications (apps) abound that allow children to listen to stories, draw creatively, or experiment with beginning writing. Children can investigate, compare, and develop problem-solving skills. They can explore shapes, colors, and lines, much like coloring. Children can play computer games where they learn to manipulate the keys and mouse or tap on a multitouch mobile device, thus using fine-motor skills and hand-eye coordination. Use lap keyboards with large letters to help children learn keyboarding. If used with discretion, computers and multitouch mobile devices can be useful tools in the classroom. They can contribute to cognitive and social development when used in developmentally appropriate ways that enhance learning. They do not replace play and hands-on activities, but they are additional means of helping children to explore, create, and communicate (NAEYC and FRC 2012).

CLOSING THOUGHTS

Emerging literacy competence begins with exposing infants and toddlers to words in a continuous stream of task-centered talking. They hear words in songs and nursery rhymes and are exposed to books. Early attempts at communication merge into beginning expressive language as words take on meaning. Parents and teachers build on this early language foundation with a literacy-rich atmosphere for preschoolers. The task-centered talking is augmented with thought-provoking, open-ended questions and discussion of interesting ideas. Books abound, and not only are they read to children, but they are used to expand ideas with a variety of activities that promote creativity and spark imaginations. Children are challenged in a variety of interesting ways to increase their knowledge and curiosity. Self-motivation becomes a primary force to learn using all their talents and modalities. Adults model writing and assist children in expressing their thoughts in print. Children's early literacy experimentation is valued. As preparation for more formal education, the early childhood classroom builds on previous cognition and elevates it to a new level, helping each child reach his full potential.

chapter 9

Lessons to Be Learned from Brain Research

We can compare brain development with the cycle of the bamboo plant. Underground rhizomes, or thickened plant stems, establish a complicated root system. Only after years of development do the first stems sprout above the ground. In a similar way, only through experiences in the surrounding environment can the brain develop a sophisticated system of synaptic connections between neurons. During the early years, the child is exposed to an enormous amount of information. The infant, and then the toddler, listens to many spoken words before beginning to understand the language. Just like the bamboo plant that is sending roots underground that can't be seen, the child's brain is making thousand of connections relating to all the language she hears.

This proliferation of synapses allows messages to be sent to all parts of the brain from input garnered by the senses. No one can see the learning that is taking place every moment. It suddenly surfaces as the child says the first word or takes an initial step, just like it takes a long time before the first green shoot pushes to the surface. A child is taking in a momentous amount of information before he is able to use the knowledge during tasks.

In the last twenty-five years, a new science arose that changed the entire way we view young children and how they learn. Modern imaging equipment enabled doctors and scientists to see the brain in action. No longer did parents and teachers need to speculate about how children develop, grow, and acquire knowledge. Suddenly the facts showed that children's brains are developing connections at a rapid rate, and experiences and environment play a major role in how learning takes place in the first five years of life. Brain research confirmed that the adults in children's lives can help children reach their full potential.

Today brain research is changing rapidly as scientists figure out new ways to view the brain while information is being learned. Future research may lead to drastic differences in understanding the way the brain relays information. This implies that anyone who interacts with young children on a daily basis needs to read and keep current on discoveries about how children learn and how memory can be strengthened. It also means we must be diligent not to let misinformation confuse what we are doing. Because biological research has confirmed that the early years are the important ones, many commercial enterprises are trying to cash in. Television advertisements shout the value of food additives to "boost" brain power. Expensive games and curricula claim to teach children better than an interactive environment. Some charlatans make up brain facts to support their theories and products. Without knowing how young children learn best, some people make recommendations about how to speed up or increase learning and development (Lally 1998). We must be wise consumers. If it sounds better than anything ever thought of, it probably isn't true.

THE IMPORTANT EARLY YEARS

Recent brain research has confirmed what educators have proposed for many years: children learn rapidly in the first few years of life. Growth and development depend on both the genetic makeup of the child and the type of environment surrounding the child. The love and nurturing of a trusted adult makes a difference. Fulfilling the physical, emotional, social, and intellectual needs of a child makes a difference. An enriched atmosphere full of exciting and stimulating experiences helps each child use brain power to the fullest. Together these attributes in the child's life ensure that the child will succeed and be ready for school, society, and life. Good quality early care and education gives every child the right start. Brain science has demonstrated the influence the early years have on a person for the rest of her life.

One of the most important messages in brain research is that we can't wait and see what will happen as children grow older. During the first five years, development occurs at a rapid pace, and when milestones are not met during the windows of opportunity, problems may arise. When a child exhibits abnormal development, there should be no delay in getting help. We know that early intervention is best for children at risk. If they are not receiving stimuli or not correctly processing stimuli, delays will likely increase. If you're concerned about a child's development, work with the parents and seek intervention from professionals who can evaluate and define what the child needs.

Some parents of children with developmental delays not only feel personal guilt but sometimes experience a feeling of hopelessness that the delays

are irreversible. Their fears must be handled gently as caregivers observe the child and make recommendations for an evaluation. It is vitally important that the caregivers possess the knowledge and skills needed to tell the truth yet help parents retain hope. Don't hesitate to consult community services for help. Early care and education personnel should not be making diagnoses. Instead, seek out an early childhood specialist who can assess the child's development, pinpoint the problem, and make recommendations for intervention. The best part of brain research is that we now have more knowledge to help children experiencing developmental delays or physical and learning problems. No matter what the problem is, we can't give up! We must still look for ways to help children. Remarkable things can happen.

We know that the brain is very plastic at a young age. Often one part of the brain takes over for an injured part. New neural pathways can be created by early intervention and an enriched environment. Infants born to drug-addicted mothers respond to nurturing; some neglected children thrive after massive environmental intervention. Stroke victims in their eighties can retrain the brain with hard work. Early intervention may be able to teach very young children to use different parts of the brain. Young children might need different techniques and more attention, but they can make strides with a specialist providing early intervention.

Early care and education providers can advocate for best practices to ensure all children have the best opportunities to learn and develop. Remind parents of the harm smoking and alcohol have on the developing child's brain during pregnancy. Secondhand smoke is bad for the health of all children. Asthma and other health problems can be traced back to exposure to cigarette smoke. And asthma is the number one reason children miss school due to a chronic condition (US EPA 2010). If children are home sick, they are not at school learning. Reminding families of the danger of shaking an infant and providing information on secondhand smoke can help children grow successfully. Supply helmets as children ride tricycles and wagons, and encourage their use at home. Teach seat belt safety to both children and their families. The brain is too vital to allow preventable delays and injuries.

Many hardworking parents of typically developing children worry that their hectic lifestyle is having a detrimental effect on their child's readiness for kindergarten. Pressure to have children excel academically limits child-centered play. Just sitting down to discuss the events of the day is difficult for people trying to balance a full workday and home responsibilities. Help families by suggesting games that can be played in the car that not only support academics but that also help children be creative. Reinforcing the notion of routines, including bedtime stories, is also helpful.

Share the numerous activities in this book with joy and enthusiasm. Communicate that every waking minute a child is learning. Parents don't have to stop and sit down to teach. Children can learn an immense amount while accompanying parents on errands, shopping, and working around the house. Help parents understand the importance of the child's contribution to family chores, which must match their age and maturation level. All of these experiences provide learning. This will help alleviate the worry and any guilt parents may have (Ginsburg 2007).

USING BRAIN RESEARCH

The most important lesson to be learned from neurobiology is that parents and teachers need to provide a stimulating, enriched environment every day if children are to reach their full potential. Each day, all the senses must be engaged in a way that motivates young children to learn. Each day should present excitement and achievable challenges. When a child feels nurtured and loved, when social skills are encouraged, proficiency will be easier for the child. This book was written as a reference book of activities to enrich environments for young children. I have provided ideas for indoors and out, for home and school. Parents, teachers, family members, and caregivers might choose to add one idea a week to enhance the child's surroundings. Mark those activities that the child enjoys so they can be repeated often. Children like repetition. Engaging in the same task many times puts the skills involved into permanent memory. Each time the child approaches the same activity, she finds familiarity but also a challenge. A different day provides a new prospective to the task. The learning builds as the child masters certain skills and finds new and creative ways to participate again.

With all this information about brain formation, what can be surmised about daily activities? What should children experience to foster the best brain development? Children need activities that

help them use their brain potential. The environment must be stimulating, challenging, and one in which the children's minds and interests are actively engaged. Children learn when their bodies and minds interact with actual objects. They gain knowledge by exploring and manipulating items in their environments. Adults narrate and illuminate what children see, hear, feel, and smell by using task-centered talking. They ask questions that elicit thinking and problem solving. Parents and teachers give children the skills they need to socialize with others, control their emotions, and creatively approach learning. Remember, for the brain to move information into long-term memory, children need to have a variety of activities that clarify information, give information meaning, and provide interesting and unique practice.

How is this done? By creating many experiences in a stress-free environment where children move and play with a variety of items. Caring, nurturing adults communicate with the children, challenging and asking them to think, talk, and use their senses. Children learn to problem solve and make hypotheses in a safe environment. With brain-compatible learning, children's brains are making connections, storing information, and helping them reach their full potential.

Look at the appropriateness of each activity for the age and stage of development of the individual

child. Does it activate at least one of the child's senses? Does it address the child's emotional and social stage? Are you providing a balance of activities from each section of this book? Make this book work for you on an ongoing basis. Then its creation will have been a success!

Glossary

auditory discrimination: The ability to discriminate between sounds using the sense of hearing.

axon: The middle part of a neuron. A long tube that transmits chemicals and electrical impulses from one end of the nerve cell to the other.

axon terminal: The end of the neuron or nerve cell that sends out chemicals and electrical impulses.

brain-compatible learning: Putting together knowledge of the brain with knowledge of what a child needs to create a learning atmosphere that is right for each child.

brain stem: The part of the brain connected to the spinal cord. It controls basic life functions like breathing, blood pressure, and digestion.

cerebral cortex or cortex: The part of the brain that stores information where learning takes place.

cortisol: A hormone released when a person experiences stress. It is also known as the stress hormone.

curriculum: The plan for a day; everything a child does in a day.

dendrites: The fingerlike extensions at the end of the axon that receive the electrical impulses and chemicals produced by the axon terminal.

developmentally appropriate: Correct for the age and developmental level of the child or children.

domains: Social, emotional, cognitive, language, and physical learning.

electrochemical messages: Chemicals, hormones, and electrical impulses sent out from neurons that affect neuron communication in the brain.

emotional intelligence: Having control of one's emotions.

experience chart: A sequential diary of an activity or experience children engage in during a period of time, usually documented on a large piece of paper.

fight-or-flight response: Feeling the need to attack or run away.

fine arts: Painting, sculpting, acting, puppetry.

fine-motor: The skill of using and controlling the small muscles in the hands and fingers.

firing of neurons: The point at which a neuron becomes so stimulated by a chemical or electrical input that it releases chemical or electrical impulses to other nerves.

gene: The genetic component inherited from biological parents.

glial cells: Brain cells that bring nourishment to the other cells and remove waste.

gross-motor: The large muscles in legs and arms.

hand-eye coordination: Moving the eyes along with the hands to perform a task.

hardwired: A term meaning the cells are permanently connected when the child is born.

hemisphere: Halves of the brain that are connected in the middle by a bundle of nerve cells.

infant: A child from birth to walking.

kinesthetic: The sixth sense of knowing where the body is in space.

limbic system: A part of the brain located above the brain stem that controls emotions.

melatonin: A hormone that helps regulate sleep.

mirror neurons: Specialized brain cells that fire and lead people to imitate others.

MRI: Magnetic resonance imaging; a noninvasive procedure that allows scientists to see the structure of the brain.

multiple intelligences: Howard Gardner's theory that individuals have unique strengths.

myelin: A fatty insulation that coats the axon and protects the neuron. It helps electrical signals flow down the axon.

nature: The influences that a child has from his genetic makeup.

neuron: A single nerve cell in the brain.

neuroplasticity: The brain's ability to reorganize neural pathways.

neurotransmitters: Chemicals that transmit messages from one neuron to another across synapses

nurture: The influence on development from adults and the surrounding environment.

parallel play: Young children playing next to each other but not interacting.

PET scan: Positron emission tomography scan, A noninvasive look at the cellular activity in the body.

predictable book: A story that repeats itself in a manner that children can easily learn.

prekindergarten: The year before a child enters kindergarten.

preschooler: A child who is thirty-six months to sixty months in age.

pruning: The process whereby the brain discards synaptic connections that are not being used and are weak.

receptors: The areas in a dendrite that accept neurotransmitters.

self-esteem: Feeling good about yourself and having confidence in your own abilities.

senses: Hearing, sight, taste, touch, smell, and kinesthetic.

sensitive period: Maria Montessori's description of the best period to learn new skills.

serotonin: A chemical that regulates mental and emotional well-being, controls motor function, regulates blood pressure, and controls hormonal function—90 percent of this chemical is found in the gut.

spinal cord: The nerve cells that connect the brain stem to the rest of the body.

synapse: The tiny space between neurons where neurotransmitters pass from one neuron to the next.

tantrum: Out-of-control display of sad emotions; includes kicking, screaming, and crying.

task-centered talking: Defined by Dr. David Sousa as a running description of what the child sees, hears, tastes, and feels throughout the day.

toddler: A mobile child to thirty-six months.

use it or lose it: If neurons are not used or stimulated, they are pruned and knowledge is lost.

window of opportunity: The optimal time to learn a skill. (*See also* "sensitive period.")

wired: The process of connecting one neuron to another through a series of synapses so they can communicate and work in tandem.

References

AACAP (American Academy of Child and Adolescent Psychiatry). 2011. "Children and TV Violence." *Facts for Families*, no. 13 (March).

AAP (American Academy of Pediatrics). 2011a. "Early Childhood Adversity, Toxic Stress, and the Role of the Pediatrician: Translating Developmental Science into Lifelong Health." Policy statement. *Pediatrics* 129 (1): e224–31. http://pediatrics.aappublications.org/content /129/1/e224.full.html.

———. 2011b. "Media Use by Children Younger Than 2 Years." Policy statement. *Pediatrics* 128 (5): 1–6. doi:10.1542/peds.2011-1753.

American SIDS Institute. 2009. "Reducing the Risk of SIDS." www.sids.org/nprevent.htm.

Bodrova, Elena. 2008."Make Believe Play versus Academic Skills: A Vygotskian Approach to Today's Dilemma of Early Childhood Education." *European Early Childhood Education Research Journal* 16 (3): 357–69. http://dx.doi .org/10.1080/13502930802291777.

Brazelton, T. Berry. 1992. *Working and Caring*. Boston: Da Capo Press.

———. 2006. *Touchpoints: Your Child's Emotional and Behavioral Development*. Rev. ed. Reading, MA: Addison-Wesley.

Carew, Thomas J., Michael Goldberg, and Eve Marder. 2008. "Mirror Neurons." *Brain Briefings*, November. www.sfn.org/index.aspx?pagename =brainBriefings_MirrorNeurons&print=on.

Carnegie Task Force on Meeting the Needs of Children. 1994. *Starting Points: Meeting the Needs of Our Youngest Children*. New York: Carnegie Corporation of New York.

Caron, Albert J., Rose F. Caron, and Darla J. MacLean. 1988. "Infant Discrimination of Naturalistic Emotional Expressions: The Role of Face and Voice." *Child Development* 59 (3): 504–16.

CDC (Centers for Disease Control and Prevention). 2011. "Nutrition, Physical Activity, and Obesity." Last modified October 17. www.cdc.gov /Features/ObesityAndKids.

Chalufour, Ingrid, and Karen Worth. 2004. *Building Structures with Young Children*. St. Paul, MN: Redleaf Press.

Chugani, Harry T. 2004. "Fine-Tuning the Baby Brain." The Dana Foundation. www.dana.org /news/cerebrum/detail.aspx?id=1228.

Chugani, Harry T., Michael E. Behen, Otto Muzik, Csaba Juhász, Ferenc Nagy, and Diane C. Chugani. 2001. "Local Brain Functional Activity Following Early Deprivation: A Study of Postinstitutionalized Romanian Orphans." *NeuroImage* 14 (October): 1290–301.

Copple, Carol, and Sue Bredekamp, eds. 2009. *Developmentally Appropriate Practice in Early Childhood Programs Serving Children from Birth through Age 8*. 3rd ed. Washington, DC: National Association for the Education of Young Children.

Doheny, Kathleen. 2004. "It's Never Too Early to Teach Kids the Activity Habit." *USA Today*, November 5. www.usatoday.com/news/health/2004-11-05-active_x.htm.

Drew, Walter F., and Baji Rankin. 2004. "Promoting Creativity for Life Using Open-Ended Materials." *Young Children* 59 (4): 38–45. Washington DC: National Association for the Education of Young Children.

Elkind, David. 2001a. *The Hurried Child: Growing Up Too Fast Too Soon.* Lavonia, MI: Addison Wesley Longman Publishing.

———. 2001b. "Much Too Early." *Education Matters*, Summer, 9–15.

Frost, Joe L., Dorothy Justice Sluss, Olga S. Jarrett, and Peggy O'Neill-Wagner. 2007. *Investigating Play in the 21st Century: Play and Culture Studies.* Lanham, MD: Rowman and Littlefield.

Gardner, Howard. 1983. *Frames of the Mind: The Theory of Multiple Intelligences.* New York: Basic Books.

———. 1999. *Intelligence Reframed: Multiple Intelligences for the 21st Century.* New York: Basic Books.

Ginsburg, Kenneth R. 2007. "The Importance of Play in Promoting Healthy Child Development and Maintaining Strong Parent-Child Bonds." *Pediatrics* 119 (1): 182–91.

Goleman, Daniel. 2012. "ECT Interview: Daniel Goleman Talks about Emotional Intelligence." *Early Childhood Today.* Scholastic, Inc. Accessed March 22. www.scholastic.com/teachers/article/ect-interview-daniel-goleman-talks-about-emotional-intelligence.

Gregory, Gayle H., and Terence Parry. 2006. *Designing Brain-Compatible Learning.* Thousand Oaks, CA: Corwin Press.

Heiting, Gary. 2010. "Your Infant's Visual Development." All About Vision. www.allaboutvision.com/parents/infants.htm.

Helm, Judy Harris, and Lilian G. Katz. 2001. *Young Investigators: The Project Approach in the Early Years.* Washington, DC: National Association for the Education of Young Children.

Iacoboni, Marco. 2008. "The Mirror Neuron Revolution: Explaining What Makes Humans Social." *Mind Matters,* July 1. http://www.scientificamerican.com/article.cfm?id=the-mirror-neuron-revolut.

Jensen, Eric. 2005. *Teaching with the Brain in Mind.* Rev. ed. Alexandria, VA: Association for Supervision and Curriculum Development.

Lally, Ronald. 1998. "Brain Research, Infant Learning, and Child Care Curriculum." *Child Care Information Exchange*, no. 121 (May/June): 45–66.

MacDonald, Ann. 2007. "Brain Development in Childhood—The Dana Guide." The Dana Foundation. www.dana.org/news/brainhealth/detail.aspx?id=10054.

Maria, Bernard. 2001. "Building a Better Brain." Gainesville, FL: University of Florida College of Medicine.

Mayo Foundation for Medical Education and Research. 2011. "Sudden Infant Death Syndrome." Last modified October 21. www.mayoclinic.com/health/sudden-infant-death-syndrome/DS00145/DSECTION=prevention.

NAEYC (National Association for the Education of Young Children). 2008. "Teacher-Child Ratio within Group Sizes." NAEYC Accreditation. www.naeyc.org/files/academy/file/Teacher-Child_Ratio_Chart_9_16_08.pdf.

NAEYC (National Association for the Education of Young Children) and FRC (Fred Rogers Corporation). 2012. *Technology and Interactive Media as Tools in Early Childhood Programs Serving Children from Birth through Age 8.* Position statement. Washington, DC: NAEYC. www.naeyc.org/files/naeyc/file/positions/PS_technology_WEB2.pdf.

NAEYC (National Association for the Education of Young Children) and IRA (International Reading Association). 2005. *Where We Stand on Learning to Read and Write: Developmentally Appropriate Practices for Young Children.* Position statement. Washington, DC: NAEYC. www.naeyc.org/files/naeyc/file/positions/WWSSLearningToReadAndWriteEnglish.pdf.

NAEYC (National Association for the Education of Young Children) and NCTM (National Council of Teachers of Mathematics). 2010.

Early Childhood Mathematics: Promoting Good Beginnings. Position statement. Reston, VA: NCTM.

Paul, Annie Murphy. 2010. *Origins: How the Nine Months before Birth Shape the Rest of Our Lives.* New York: Free Press.

Perry, Bruce D. 2003. "Neurodevelopment and the Neurophysiology of Trauma: Conceptual Considerations for Clinical Work with Maltreated Children." Florida Agency for Workforce Innovations Conference, Orlando, FL.

————. 2006. "Applying Principles of Neurodevelopment to Clinical Work with Maltreated and Traumatized Children: The Neurosequential Model of Therapeutics" In *Working with Traumatized Youth in Child Welfare*, edited by Nancy Boyd Web, 27–51. New York: Guilford Press.

————. 2011. "Aggression and Violence: The Neurobiology of Experience." Accessed August 28. http://teacher.scholastic.com/professional /bruceperry/aggression_violence.htm.

Phelps, Pamela. 2003. Early Childhood Association of Florida Conference Keynote, Orlando, FL.

Pitcher, Evelyn G., Sylvia G. Feinburg, and David Alexander. 2000. *Helping Young Children Learn.* Rev. ed. Columbus, OH: Merrill Publishing.

Polak, Natasha. 2009. "Baby and Child Movement: Exercise for Everyone." Baby Zone. www .babyzone.com/mom_dad/fitness_nutrition /article/baby-child-exercise.

Rideout, Victoria, Elizabeth Hamel, and the Kaiser Family Foundation. 2006. *The Media Family: Electronic Media in the Lives of Infants, Toddlers, Preschoolers, and Their Parents.* Menlo Park, CA: Kaiser Family Foundation.

Salimpoor, Valorie N., Mitchel Benovoy, Kevin Larcher, Alain Dagher, and Robert J. Zatorre. 2011. "Anatomically Distinct Dopamine Release during Anticipation and Experience of Peak Emotion to Music." *Nature Neuroscience* 14:257–62.

Schiller, Pam. 2010. "Early Brain Development Research Review and Update." *Exchange*, no. 196 (November/December): 26–30.

Shonkoff, Jack P., and Deborah A. Phillips, eds. 2000. *From Neurons to Neighborhoods: The Science of Early Childhood Development.* Washington, DC: National Academy Press.

Shore, Rebecca. 2002. *Baby Teacher: Nurturing Neural Networks from Birth to Age Five.* Lanham, MD: Scarecrow Press.

Singer, Jayne. 2007. "The Brazelton Touchpoints Approach to Infants and Toddlers in Care: Foundation for a Lifetime of Learning and Loving." *Dimensions of Early Childhood* 35 (3): 4–10.

Society for Neuroscience. 2008. "Mirror Neurons." *Brain Briefings*, November.

Sohn, Emily. 2010. "Mommy Brain: It's Not What You Think." *Discovery News*, October 22. http://news.discovery.com/human/mommy -brain-maternal-changes.html.

Sousa, David. 1998. "The Ramifications of Brain Research." *School Administrator*, January. www.aasa.org/SchoolAdministratorArticle .aspx?id=15152.

————. 2006. *How the Brain Learns.* Thousand Oaks, CA: Corwin Press.

————. 2008. *How the Brain Learns Mathematics.* Thousand Oaks, CA: Corwin Press.

US EPA (United States Environmental Protection Agency). 2010. *Managing Asthma in the School Environment.* Washington, DC: US EPA. http://epa.gov/iaq/schools/pdfs/publications /managing_asthma.pdf.

Willis, Clarissa A., and Pam Schiller. 2011. "Preschoolers' Social Skills Steer Life Success." *Young Children* 66 (1): 42–49.

Zero To Three. 2011. "FAQ's on the Brain." www .zerotothree.org/child-development/brain -development/faqs-on-the-brain.html.

Photography Credits

Thanks to the following photographers: Faith Alexander, Jenny Baird, Jennifer Barrera, Judy Bayless, Judi Miller Bruckner, Jodi Delany, Tarah Fred, Suzanne Gellens, Jayne Hafer, Darla Hoffman, Kathy Kourapis, Ginger Lee, Heather Locklear, Eunice Lopez, Donna Lovelace, Lindsay Marchisello, Bernard Maria, Kelly McGuire, Tuan Nguyen, Marlene Ramos, Marian Rutkowski, Ashley Terry, Ashley VanHoose, Susie Wells, Tasha Williams, and Christine Wozniak.

Thanks to these child care programs for the photographs: Academy to Success, Tampa, FL; After Kicks, Tampa, FL; Bayshore Baptist Preschool, Tampa, FL; Discovery Days Preschool, Sarasota, FL; Forty Carrots Family Center, Sarasota, FL; Hillsborough Community College Child Care Center—Ybor, Tampa, FL; Kids Planet Preschool, St. Petersburg, FL; Methodist Children's Village, Jacksonville, FL; Mid-Florida Community Services, Head Start Volusia County, FL; New Dimensions Learning Center, Jacksonville, FL; North East Focal Point Intergenerational Child Care Center, Deerfield Beach, FL; The Oaks Early Learning Academy, Jacksonville, FL; Play Care Daycare and Preschool, Tampa, FL; Precious People Learning Center, Palm Harbor, FL; Riverview High School Teen Parent Program, Sarasota, FL; Rosa Valdez Child Care Center, Tampa, FL; Sarasota County Technical Institute Tech Tots, Sarasota, FL; and Sarasota Memorial Hospital Child Care Center, Sarasota, FL.

Index

videos, viewing, 36–37
violence, television viewing and, 36
Viorst, Judith, 125
visual system. *See* eye problems; sight, sense of
vocabulary
    acquisition of, 76–77
    preschool activities for building, 126–27
volcanoes, creating, 108

W

Waber, Bernard, 92
walkers, 57
walking, development of, 18, 54, 55
walks, 17, 23, 108
water and sand areas, 23, 105–6
water play, 35, 67, 105–6
websites, selecting resources and materials, 36–37
We're Going on a Bear Hunt (Rosen and Oxenbury), 125
"Wheels on the Bus, The," 84, 118
"Where Is Thumbkin?," 58
"Where's the Baby?," 78
Where's Waldo (Handford), 124
whispering, 15, 46
Whistle for Willie (Keats), 126
windows of opportunity, 11, 138, 142
wiring, neuronal
    biology of, 8, 69, 137

development of, 9–12, 69–70
emotional development and, 30
neuroplasticity, 9, 138, 142
    See also brain development
woodworking activities, 67
word awareness, teaching, 121–22, 131–32, 133–34
word boxes, 134
word walls, 133–34
working memory, 86–87
writing skill development
    experience charts, 134, 141
    infants and toddlers, 78–79
    initial attempts, 135
    journals, 134–35
    project approach, 135
    teaching approaches, 121–22, 134
    writing tables, 128–29

Y

"Yankee Doodle," 83, 118
Yuk Soup (Crowley), 125

Z

Zion, Gene, 129
Zoo Book, The (Pfloog), 134
zoos, visiting, 78, 134

About the Author

Suzanne Gellens taught deaf and hearing-impaired children for fourteen years after graduating with a master's degree in speech and hearing from the University of Kansas. She came to Florida and taught normally developing children for twenty-five years, specializing in working with children two to six years of age. She established and was the director of Temple Emanu-El Early Learning Center in Sarasota, Florida, for seventeen years. The center became accredited by the National Association for the Education of Young Children and had a preschool, kindergarten, and first grade. In 1996, Gellens became the executive director of the Florida Association for the Education of Young Children, a nonprofit organization serving 3,500 early care and education providers throughout the state of Florida.

Gellens is past president of the Sarasota Association on Children Under Six, the Early Childhood Association of Florida, and the Southern Early Childhood Association. She serves on numerous committees and task forces focusing on early childhood services in Florida. She conducts workshops on early childhood topics and has published articles on all aspects of early care and education. Gellens resides in Tampa, Florida, near her two daughters and three grandchildren.